MORE PRAISE FOR

I Will Not Die an Unlived Life

"*I Will Not Die An Unlived Life* is a moving book in the best sense of the word: read it with your mind descended into your heart, and it will move you closer to living life to its fullest."

—PARKER J. PALMER, author of
Let Your Life Speak and *The Courage to Teach*

"Dawna Markova has long been a passionate and clear voice in the life of our tribe. In her latest book, *I Will Not Die an Unlived Life*, she shares and models the essence of skillful befriending: befriending the unknown guest who lives within, befriending each other, and befriending the world we are shaping. This book is a personal laboratory that allows us to glimpse our common seeds."

—MARK NEPO, author of
The Book of Awakening and *Acre of Light*

"The vitality and passion that exudes from *I Will Not Die An Unlived Life* promises to bring inspiration to every fortunate soul who reads it. Dawna's profoundly personal yet universal insights compel each of us to discover the tender heart of our own humanity, to realize the promise and potential of our precious lives, and to awaken a fierce commitment to live in a way we will be proud of when inevitably it is our time to die."

—JOEL LEVEY, PH.D. and MICHELLE LEVEY, M.A.,
authors of: *Living in Balance* and *Simple Meditation & Relaxation*

"There is no deeper, nor more challenging,
question than how we will live our lives. It confronts us
at a collective as well as an intimate level. While we are
waiting for the circumstances of our lives to match our expectations, life is waiting for us to release our expectations and
realize the possibility that exists now, regardless of our
circumstances.Only then, as Dawna Markova's book shows
so beautifully, does anger become compassion and fear
melt, to reveal courage, passion and love."

—PETER M. SENGE, author of *The Dance of Change*
and *The Fifth Discipline*

"Like the lotus on its cover, *I Will Not Die an Unlived Life*
by Dawna Markova is potent with meaning and graceful
in form.... In it Markova offers fresh approaches to
bring to the exploration of meaning in our lives."

—MAGGIE OMAN SHANNON, editor of *Prayers for Healing*

I Will Not Die an Unlived Life

Other books by DAWNA MARKOVA

The Art of the Possible
The Open Mind
No Enemies Within
Learning Unlimited, coauthored
with Anne Powell
An Unused Intelligence, coauthored
with Andy Bryner
How Your Child Is Smart, coauthored
with Anne Powell
coeditor, *Random Acts of Kindness*
contributor, *Fabric of the Future;*
For She Is the Tree of Life

I Will Not Die an Unlived Life

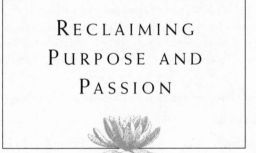

RECLAIMING
PURPOSE AND
PASSION

DAWNA MARKOVA

Foreword by Justine and Michael Toms

CONARI PRESS
Berkeley, California

Conari Press books are distributed by Publishers Group West.

ISBN: 1-57324-101-6

Cover Photography: Courtesy of Photonica, Fumio Otsuka © 1992
Cover Design: Ame Beanland
Book Design: Suzannne Albertson
Author Photo: Hollie Noble

LIBRARY OF CONGRESS CATALOGING-IN-PUBLICATION DATA

Markova, Dawna, 1942–
      I will not die an unlived life : reclaiming purpose and passion /
Dawna Markova.
            p.   cm.
      ISBN 1-57324-101-6
            1. Self-perception. 2. Markova, Dawna, 1942– I. Title.
      BF697.5.S43 M27 2000
      158.1—dc21   00-009527

Printed in the United States of America on recycled paper.

00 01 02 03   Data Repro   10 9 8 7 6 5 4 3 2 1

This book is dedicated to Mary Jane Ryan and those

who insist on breaking free of the limitations of their previous history,

who wish to love the life they live, live a life they can love,

and

who are committed to serving the best of what can be possible.

I Will Not Die an Unlived Life

IV

Living On Path: Landscapes of the Spirit 137

EPILOGUE

The Seasons of Renewal: A Living Landscape 183

Foreword

WE ARE LIVING IN TIMES OF OLYMPIC LEVELS OF DISTRACTION and busyness. Most of the Western world is caught up in doing, doing, doing-we have become trained *to do* in order *to have* so that maybe in some distant time we can *be.* This is all backward, from the point of view of the soul. As we become quiet enough to listen to the longings of the soul, we may arrive at a deeper level of activity in our lives. We may first live the being and from that will emerge the doing. This is clearly the experience of Dawna Markova, who is a master of the essential questions, such as, "What am I more curious about than afraid of?" She stops our analytical minds and takes us into our heartminds, where the soul resides and where we can connect with our inner wisdom.

When reading this book, from the beginning we were reminded of Anne Morrow Lindbergh's classic *Gift from the Sea,* which continues to be passed on from generation to generation for more than half a century. *I Will Not Die an Unlived Life* is just such a book for the new century. We found ourselves reading it aloud to one another, highlighting and underlining it so extensively that it is spiderwebby with marks, exclamation points, and notes.

Never have the words *slow down* been so desperately needed as they are now. We laughed out loud at Dawna's story of doing nothing for forty-five minutes and looking around as if "waiting for the Time Police to arrest [her] for being nonproductive."

Markova asks brilliant questions as she gently challenges us to exit the fast lane and move into the slow river of wonder, which summons us to our true passion. She catches our logical minds and prompts us to remember, "Why are we here?" She stimulates us to ask essential questions, have more conversations, and tell more stories. She speaks the language of poetry, questions, story-telling, and deep reflection.

I Will Not Die an Unlived Life takes us on a journey of "what it would mean to live fully, sensually alive, and passionately, on purpose." She reminds us of what we already intuit: "My head is stuffed with knowledge, but something in me is still starving." We are compelled to set down the book and do some soul searching of our own. It is a book meant to be savored, read and re-read, then shared with others, and used as a guide for retreats. This surely will come after being so intimately connected with Markova's journey into herself. Anyone on a spiritual quest, seeking to discover their own deep wisdom, and uncover their "calling" will be enriched and energized in a powerful and gentle way, just as we were.

by Justine and Michael Toms, cofounders of New Dimensions Broadcasting Network, cocreators of the internationally syndicated "New Dimensions" radio series, and coauthors of *True Work: Doing What You Love and Loving What You Do*

I

Living Wide Open:
Landscapes of the Mind

I will not die an unlived life.
I will not live in fear
of falling or catching fire.
I choose to inhabit my days,
to allow my living to open me,
to make me less afraid,
more accessible;
to loosen my heart
until it becomes a wing,
a torch, a promise.
I choose to risk my significance,
to live so that which came to me as seed
goes to the next as blossom,
and that which came to me as blossom,
goes on as fruit.

CHAPTER 1

A Second Innocence

I WROTE THIS POEM THE NIGHT MY FATHER DIED WITH A SHRUG. His heart was hollow and vacant of dreams. He was convinced he didn't matter.

We were in very different places. He lived with my mother in a condo in the heat of Hollywood, Florida, and I lived in an icy valley outside of Norwich, Vermont. One day I was in the office where I practiced psychotherapy. Linda was trying to decide whether or not to divorce Jim, her abusive husband. I was listening intently as she spoke, when suddenly, behind her, there was my father, or what could be described as a shimmering hologram of my father. He stood, staring at me, and then shrugged. He reached toward me. The jade pinky ring he always wore on his right hand slipped past his knuckle and fell to the floor.

Linda didn't notice anything out of the ordinary. Tears fell as she talked about Jim beating her up. My father beat me up, so I understood why she was crying. I reached over to let her know she was not alone. When I shifted my gaze back behind her, my translucent father was gone.

Later that evening, I called my mother, who had just returned from the hospital. She told me in a trembling voice that my father had passed away a few hours before, when she stepped out to the cafeteria to get a cup of coffee. I wept myself to sleep. The tears broke through me the way the frozen rivers in Vermont break open in the spring. Rivers of reaching, rivers of yearning. I floated to sleep on a surging tide of grief.

I awoke when the night was at its very blackest, feeling as if I were not only the river, but also the riverbed. I was soil, fertile, deep, open. In that moment, I understood something, without reason or explanation. I stared at my right hand. It was moving, as if it were a green plant reaching for light. I watched it turn on the old brass lamp next to my bed. I watched it reach for my favorite blue Waterman fountain pen. I watched it stretch toward my worn red leather journal. I watched it write, as if taking dictation from someone other than me, "I will not die an unlived life...."

I got out of bed, carrying my journal over to the old mahogany desk that had been my father's. I could feel the river swelling in my heart. As I sat down, it flowed out of my hand.

The tears had turned to ink. The words were a bridge across an abyss my father could not cross. They were his blessing to me.

When I was ten, I read about Helen Keller and Joan of Arc and Wonder Woman, and for a few years I believed that if I did what my heart told me to do, I could help create less suffering in the world, and maybe even a little more joy. When people asked me what I wanted to be when I grew up, I told them I wanted to make the world a better place.

Grownups always had the same reaction—they snickered, patted me on the head, and asked, "But how are you going to make money, Sweetie?" The pats and questions didn't stop my aspiration, but they did drive it deeper and deeper in me until it was a lonely firefly on a late August evening.

Like most kids, I had a secret place. I used to skip to the reservoir behind our house and hide in the reeds that grew on its shore. I loved to pick just the right pebble, put all my good feelings into it, and toss it in the clear green water. I watched that good feeling ripple until they touched all the shores.

I could very easily imagine, sitting there with my chin tucked snug under my knees, that some day, when I was grown up, I'd be able to create ripples of good feelings all the way to South Africa, which was about as far as I could imagine, and those ripples would make the world a better place.

When I was a woman in full stride, I was still secretly trying to make ripples. I never mentioned it to anyone else, but every once in a while, I did something just because my heart rang "yes" as if someone had tapped a secret tuning fork. Just after Nelson Mandela was elected president of South Africa, for instance, I helped organize a gathering of thirty women from around the world to explore the question, "How can we as leaders nurture ourselves while making a difference in the world?"

Women from thirty countries came to a beautiful old mansion in Oxford, England, to explore that question. The first day, my eyes kept being drawn to a woman sitting silently in a big armchair, her chocolate skin glowing in the early autumn sun, her head and body erect. She was wrapped in orange flowered fabric that reminded me of sunsets and jungles and joy. The only words she said since we began the meeting were her name, Nomathemba Luhabe, and the country she represented, South Africa.

"You guys just don't understand," Roz, one of the other facilitators explained in her thick Kiwi accent after the morning session on the second day. "Nomathemba's rhythm of speaking is completely different than you Yanks. She won't talk until we slow down and leave some space so what one person has said can be absorbed before the next person chimes in."

Roz folded her arms across her abundant chest and sat back in her chair. I tried to listen without being defensive. The five of us who had designed this conference were huddled together in a small room. We were aligned in our intention—to create supportive and unifying conversations that really mattered between women from vastly different cultures—but we had been having disagreements about how to do this almost from the beginning. Some of the static was due to the fact that we had been trying to plan this conference electronically for months, without "face time," without money, and without all of us knowing each other. But I think most of our difficulties were due to the fact that none of us really knew how to create the conditions that would support such conversations. All we knew was that they were important. If we were successful, each woman would go back to her own country and create a similar conversation with thirty of her countrywomen. We were going for the ripple effect.

That afternoon, Roz and I facilitated the session and suggested to everyone that we might try to slow things down somewhat by using a small group dialogue format, which seemed to help. But Nomathemba still didn't say a word.

We had asked people to bring a symbolic gift to share with the other women. Each night's session involved ten of us offering what we had brought for the rest of the group. The second night was my turn, but I'd forgotten to bring anything. That afternoon, a thousand ideas ran through my mind. Finally, I flounced down on the bed, and found my journal under the pillow. As I looked at the cover, an idea blossomed.

I offered my gift first that evening. My heart began to knock on the door to my mouth, as I began explaining,

"I'd like to give you the poem I wrote on the night my father died. It means a great deal to me.

"I felt so fragile and alone that night, wondering what my father's life had been about, what I had learned from him, how I could go on without him." I risked looking at the women in the circle. They were in full focus now, attentive, present. With more confidence, I went on,

"I sat with my worn journal and blue fountain pen in my lap, longing for the relief that only writing can bring me. I began to hum lullabies the way I had when I nursed my son. I felt a tingling in my breasts that I always felt when my milk let down. My hand picked up the pen and words began to flow out."

As I lifted the white piece of paper where I had written the poem, my hands began to shake the way they always do when a lot of energy runs through my body. "These words are the footprints I follow. They have led me through cancer and chaos. They remind me who I am and why I am here. Perhaps they will do the same for you."

I began to read, feeling totally still, the way I always do when I speak the poem aloud. When I finished, the silence in the room was vibrating. I stood up and went from woman to woman, giving each a handwritten copy I made that afternoon. I placed the last one in Nomathemba's brown outstretched hand, and went back to the stiff-backed chair I had been sitting on.

The silence was easy, open now. After a few minutes, I leaned forward and asked who else would like to offer a gift.

"Stop." The word resounded across the circle. Nomathemba's blazing dark eyes moved around, resting on each of us for a moment. When she turned to me, a pack of ravenous beasts inside my mind snarled about how stupid I had been to read the poem, how I had gone too fast again, how she was going to tell everyone how insensitive and rude I had been.

"I did not know who you were," she said shaking her head. "I cannot believe I was so unaware, so out of touch with the present moment that in two days I did not realize you were here."

I wanted to look behind me to see who she was talking to, but I knew there could be no one else she was addressing.

As if reading my mind she said, "You do not know me, and I have never seen you before, but I know you." She slipped her hand inside the folds of her flowing sleeve and pulled out a greeting card.

"A friend from the States sent me this card two years ago. I have been carrying it with me ever since." She held it up for me to see. I recognized it immediately. When I was staying at a retreat center in the south of France several years ago, a young woman with flashing black eyes and tangled hair approached me, introduced herself, and told me she had overhead me telling someone my name was Dawna Markova. She said she had read a poem of mine entitled, "I Will Not Die an Unlived Life" in a newsletter and wanted to put some art work with it and make it into a card if I didn't mind. I assumed she meant the kind of personal card you make to send a friend, so I agreed readily. Months later someone sent me the card she had designed, which was being produced, as was a journal, with the poem on the cover, by a California company. By now, thousands of cards and journals with the poem had been sold. When I first found out, I felt as if I had been mumbling a very private thought only to discover a microphone had secretly been placed inside my blouse and my words were being broadcast to ten thousand people in an amphitheater.

Nomathemba stood and walked deliberately into the center of the circle, her eyes locked with mine. Each step was as precise as the words which followed.

"I have been traveling from one end of my country to the other, speaking to large and small groups of women. I explain to them that if we can gather our purchasing power together, we will become a mighty political force." Her words paused, but she continued walking until she stood in front of me.

"At the end of each talk, I read this poem. Thousands and thousands of women have heard it." Nomathemba extended her hands toward me, palms up and open. Her eyes shone as she whispered, "I tell them that I will be the rich soil in which the seeds of their dreams can sprout."

I placed my hands in hers and she dropped down to her knees in front of me. I slipped off my chair onto the floor and my tears fell onto our intertwined hands. We sat like that for many moments. Finally, I spoke.

"Twenty-six years ago, when my son David was five years old, we drove around the world." I spoke directly to her, slowly, quietly. "We lived in East Africa for some time. David learned to speak Swahili and Masai. Then we drove all the way down to your country. The land was so beautiful, it made me gasp again and again. The second day we were in Jo'burg, David went to the park. The police brought him back to our apartment, because he had been playing in the section that was for black children only. They told him he was forbidden to be there, but he told them he wouldn't move to the white children's 'cage.'"

When I spoke, my voice was edged, swallowing back the broken glass of tears. "He kept asking me what he had done wrong. I tried to explain that which had no explanation." I sighed and looked at our hands for a moment, and then went on, "Finally, I knew we would have to leave. Three days later, we drove to Capetown and left on a tramp steamer to Singapore. As we pulled out of the harbor, I prayed I would find a way to come back at a time when it was safe to bring a child there, when all who were different would belong."

I heard people sniffing all around us, but I could not stop yet. I had one more message I needed to deliver.

"The gift you have given me today is immense. I have needed to withdraw, to stop working so much for a while so I can write."

I peered over my shoulder at the others in the circle and then back to Nomathemba. "The gift you give me is the awareness that I can be true to my own need to be private. At the same time, a reaching from my heart found you. In doing so, I have found my way back to South Africa. In some small, seed-like way, I have been a part of encouraging your people to risk their significance."

To say we embraced would be insufficient. The roots of who we were entwined, the earth sighed in satisfaction, and a new possibility was born.

I once read that the Nobel Prize-winning South American poet, Octavio Paz, after realizing how much of his creative energy he had used to stay out of life instead of participating in it, wrote a poem entitled *After*, as a commitment that he would no longer be in the great gift of life with hesitation, ambivalence, or reservation, and that he would no longer push life or love away. Because it so impassioned him with its truth, he read it to himself every morning and evening for the rest of his life.

Likewise, before my foot hits the floor each morning, I say the words of my poem aloud, slowly. They are the path, and the light I need to follow it. Each evening, when my feet are safely tucked into bed, I whisper the words again, in order to check whether I have lost the way, gotten crooked, or am still on path. They are how I know if my soul is leaking or burgeoning.

Twenty years living with a life-threatening disease, cancer, brings me into daily conversations with my soul. My healing has depended upon these as much or more as they have on medical expertise. I think cancer was my soul's desperate attempt to get me to pay attention to its needs for intimacy, authentic expression, creativity, and replenishing solitude. I think of cancer as a teacher that was not invited, but has come to my house to visit from time to time nonetheless. It sits on my left side whispering insistent questions that I cannot answer but still must explore: Who am I when I stop doing, when I am not a caretaker as my mother was or a boss as my father was? What have I come here to give? What is unfinished for me to learn, to experience? Am I leaving a legacy that enables others to live bigger lives than I have?

These are questions that belong to all of us. Any life crisis brings up issues of the purpose of one's life and the passion to live. But you don't have to be in a life-threatening situation to want to delve into this kind of inquiry. Some of us are called to it by numbness, fatigue, or boredom. Some of us have the sense that we're not using ourselves to the utmost. Even at their happiest moments, others feel something is missing.

After a long absence, my teacher returned a few years ago. I noticed that I was mumbling the poem each morning, forgetting it each night. The color had leeched out of my voice and the words were rote as if I had been saying, "Now I lay me down to sleep. . . ." Passion and purpose were seven-letter words in a language I had forgotten how to speak.

The past twenty years with cancer have taught me that healing happens in a thousand, ten thousand, tiny, daily gestures. Each of them has led me here now, to a six-month retreat high in the mountains of Utah, surrounded by nothing and no one so much as my own heart, mind, and soul. I came here where winter has cleared the landscape, however brutally. It's given me the chance to see myself and how I am living more clearly, to find the very ground of my being.

The poem is a candle that my soul holds out to me, requesting I find a way to remember what it is to live a life with passion, on purpose. There is only enough light to take the journey step by step, but that is all any of us really needs. This book is a paper trail of the steps as I took them, the ideas, questions, dreams, images, and experiments, the exploration through a dark wilderness of heart and mind.

I do not understand the physics of ripples. I do not know why people who have read this poem write to me from all over the world. I do not even know really if, like my child, it came through me, as well as for me. There is so much I don't know right now.

But I am sure there are many others in this particular time, who, like me, are feeling very disconnected from the world that pours forth anguish like rain. I know there are others who need to learn to live in an interdependent, diverse, ever-changing world, a world in which the unexpected is the expected, and breakdown and reconstruction of everything we know is daily fare.

My journey is no more or less important than yours. It is just the only one I can make authentically. The stories I tell are my truth only. They represent my understanding of what happened like a work of art, not a photograph. If told by anyone else, they would be different. I tell them in hope that what is true for me can reveal what could be true for you. In a way, I wrote this book as a slowly arriving letter to you, in support of your living fully alive, on purpose.

We all feel a tremendous push from the past and a compelling pull from the future to step fully into who we were meant to be. We need courage and time to reorder our priorities and consider internal exploration as important as "our career" and outward success. We need to practice the art of stripping away false notions about who we think we are so we can deal with what is real, and release anything that is deadening to our spirits. We have to learn to reconnect with ourselves so that we can stand for something that is greater than ourselves.

*W*hen we find ourselves devoid of passion and purpose, the first thing we need to do is stop. But that's not easy. The rest of the world is zooming by at full speed. Left alone with ourselves, without a project to occupy us, we can become nervous and self-critical about what we should be doing and feeling. This can be so uncomfortable that we look for any distraction rather than allowing ourselves the space to be as we are.

CHAPTER 2

How Do I Live Divided No More?

The seed that is to grow
must lose itself as seed;
And they that creep
may graduate through
chrysalis to wings.

Wilt thou then, O mortal,
cling to husks which
falsely seem to you
the self?
—WU MING FU, TWELFTH CENTURY

I AM IN A TINY LOG CABIN IN UTAH, 8,320 feet above just about everything, on a mountain knoll that is embraced by one long arm, the Wasatch Mountains, on the left and another, the Uintas on the right. I can see them encircling me from any window. I am surrounded by what Thomas Merton called "the hidden wholeness" of the natural world. I have come to this refuge because it is a safe place in which to tell myself the truth about what I feel. I am groping to understand what it might mean to truly love my life, to find out who I am beyond the economic necessities of being a mind-for-hire. I want to stop running from my own tiredness, from the fear that if I am not accomplishing something, I will disappear. My external life is so neatly organized into lists which tell me exactly what to do and how to think in order to be productive and successful, yet my soul has been withering a bit more each day.

I need to recover a rhythm in my heart that moves my body first and my mind second, that allows my soul to catch up with me. I need to take a sacred pause, as if I were a sun-warmed rock in the center of a rushing river. I need total media deprivation, so I can step back from the detail of little dots I have been thinking about analytically and absorb the whole pattern that only my wild and wide mind can perceive.

In essence, I need to come home to myself. It's not really how far I move to find my own wisdom that matters, but it's crucially important that I take myself along on the journey. I've put so much faith in accumulating knowledge, but knowledge isn't enough to heal me. The issue now is not curing my body, but healing my heart. I need to find the wisdom that helps me live with what is and move forward from there.

I need to stop. I need to stop and sip a cup of tea in the old wicker rocking chair on our deck. I need days that are a sweet and slow ceremony, walking in these mountains where the very air has nourishment, walking as if I am a person free of regrets, free of worries about what might be.

All around me, the aspen trees are shedding their dried golden leaves. I need to shed, to let go of what no longer is alive, to get bare enough to find the bones of what is important to me. I need to let go of the ways of knowing that have not, cannot, and will not take me where I want to go.

I have been living a divided life, caught too often unprotected and unprepared in the face of too much happening too often. When my friend and teacher Parker Palmer first asked the question "How do I live divided no more?", it was as if a tidal wave washed over me. What *would* it be like to give myself my own undivided attention? Put another way, who am I when I am no longer doing, no longer productive, no longer indispensable to so many others? I have to pay attention to my own attention: Where does it go, to whom, and why? Is it really possible to give all of it to one thing at a time?

I need a kind of spiritual inhalation, a spaciousness that comes when I am living from the inside out. Only in this way can I find my joy again, the tenderness I can feel toward myself and the world. *Find* is the wrong word. I don't think anyone "finds" joy. Rather, we cultivate it by searching for the preciousness of small things, the ordinary miracles, that strengthen our hearts so we can keep them open to what is difficult: delight in taking a shower or a slow walk that has no destination, in touching something soft, in noticing the one small, black bird who sings every morning from the top of the big old pine tree that guards this cabin. I need to give my attention to the simple things that give me pleasure with the same fervor I have been giving it to the complex things with which I drive myself crazy.

My mother always told me that having a family made it impossible for her to take time for herself the way her favorite author, Anne Morrow Lindbergh, did. She was too busy to read or retreat. I have brought the book *Gift from the Sea* with me. The irony is that one generation later, it is my family that is making it possible for me to retreat for six months.

There are no mirrors in this cabin except one over the bathroom sink. I want a different kind of reflection. I want to stop looking in on myself as if at a felon with the eyes of a bank camera or a soap opera star with the eyes of an audience. I want to see out, and see the images that my mind uses to think with. Each of the drawings I did this week all looked like a variation on the theme of an eye. Turn them upside down and they all looked like a breast: "See what is. No TV, no newspapers. Learn again how to nourish yourself."

This morning I read Lindbergh's words as she reflected on her life, "For it is only framed in space that beauty blooms. A candle flowers in the space of night . . . My life lacks this quality of significance, and therefore beauty, because there is so little empty space. There are so few empty pages in my engagement pad or empty hours in which to stand alone and find myself." Sipping a cup of cinnamon tea, I feel companioned. I am not the only one who ever felt lost and fragmented, asking how to remain whole when we are pulled off center by the centrifugal force of an ever-widening circle of contact and relationship.

Lindbergh used seashells to help her "think out her own particular pattern of living." I decide to look around this natural environment for similar mirrors. I begin exploring the shape of my life now through what I can find here—the pinecone I stuffed mindlessly in my pocket during a long walk yesterday.

I write a description of it in my journal: *I am hard and very dried out now, ordinary brown and made of hundreds of scales. The fall winds were so intense that I was blown down from a big old tree. The sticky stuff that held all of me together has dried out too, and I fall apart at the slightest touch, losing my shape altogether. When the snow comes, if you care enough to look closely, you'll notice that those scales are really little brown wings, and each holds a seed. The winds will carry them in many directions. Some will be eaten by birds, but some will be buried and hidden beneath the snow, dormant until the air turns warm and tender green and the world melts, ready for a grand sprouting.*

I read it aloud as if I had been describing myself, and its truth makes me feel exposed. But that is what I want. I am not interested in recovering anything that was. This time is about uncovering and discovering what is true. I go out on the deck and watch the blue of the sky deepen to let out the stars. I didn't see its beauty in such bold relief before. I didn't understand the whisper of the wind against my cheek. The big old spruce that stands behind the cabin reminds me that both of us grow by thrusting our roots into the darkness as well as our branches into the light.

The first week I was here, all I wanted to do was sleep, nap, rest, read, sleep, eat. The second week was mostly walking, writing in my journal, and making rich and earthy soups. Now the trees are bare, and the smell of snow is in the air, but it hasn't fallen yet. I can see the skeletons of the trees clearly, singly and together, as well as the ground they are rooted in. This exposed landscape gives me a chance to see my own life, the ground of my being, without distraction.

I have brought companions to this 650-square-foot refuge. There is Shaka, the Golden Retriever, who barks frequently enough to activate my imagination. There are stacks of books I have been hungry to read for months, including nature guides with the names of everything from antelope to zirconium. I've brought many pads of different papers, watercolors, and music for moods and variations: Mahler, Mozart, Schubert, Brazilian street music, Bobby McFerrin, Sweet Honey in the Rock, and everything Baroque I could find. My journal has become a paper mirror, a topographic map to my mind. It is where I go to sort out confusion and decipher the invisible. Some days, all I have been able to do is collapse into its open arms, bringing forth the most mundane junk in the world.

I am stunned to discover now that I have been sitting in front of the west window doing nothing for forty-five minutes. How long has it been since I really did absolutely nothing for three-quarters of an hour? I looked around as if waiting for the Time Police to arrest me for being nonproductive. All I have done is step into the darkness inside myself, into the silence, where I don't know how the world is made.

There were a series of incidents that blew me over the threshold into this retreat. One was something the poet David Whyte said a friend, Brother David Steindl-Rast, told him: "The antidote to exhaustion may not be rest. It may be wholeheartedness. You are so exhausted because all of the things you are doing are just busyness. There's a central core of wholeheartedness totally missing from what you're doing." Whyte said that from that moment on everything changed for him. He realized there were courageous conversations he had to have, because his work had become too small for him.

Listening, I became aware of the courageous conversations I needed to be having—with myself. But how could this be possible when I couldn't even hear myself think? In the following weeks, all around me, in the media and in corporations, I kept hearing three phrases that wouldn't leave me alone: "the meaning void," "Time is the new poverty," and "whatever" (said with a slack jaw and a shrug of limp shoulders).

How can any of us find our way to wholeheartedness in a meaning void? I knew that time was something we gave ourselves or didn't, and that "whatever" was the quickest way to soul leakage. And none of us can find meaning or wholeheartedness unless we are in a void, a void of everyone else's images and information.

My grandmother used to fast once a year for twenty-four hours during the holiday of Yom Kippur. Listening to her empty stomach growling, I asked her once why she fasted. She didn't say anything for several moments and then she replied, "You can't grab God. You just have to become empty. Then God will have a space to enter."

So many of us are afraid of meeting ourselves, alone, without distraction. We have been taught to fashion an image of who we think we are supposed to be and show that to the world. Through fear of knowing who we really are we sidestep our own destiny, which leaves us hungry in a famine of our own making. Each of us is here to give something that only we can offer, and when we avoid knowing ourselves, we end up living numb, passionless lives, disconnected from our soul's true purpose. But when you have the courage to shape your life from the essence of who you are, you ignite, becoming truly alive. This requires letting go of everything that is inauthentic. But how can you even know your truth unless you slow down, in your own quiet company? When the inner walls to your soul are graffitied with advertisements, commercials, and the opinions of everyone who has ever known and labeled you, turning inward requires nothing less than a major clean-up.

Traveling from the known to the unknown requires crossing an abyss of emptiness. We first experience disorientation and confusion. Then, if we are willing to cross the abyss in curious and playful wonder, we enter an expansive and untamed country that has its own rhythm. Time melts and thoughts become stories, music, poems, images, ideas. This is the intelligence of the heart, but by that I don't mean just the seat of our emotions. I mean a vast range of receptive and connective abilities: intuition, innovation, wisdom, creativity, sensitivity, the aesthetic, qualitative and meaning making. It is here that we uncover our purpose and passion.

The future exists only in our imaginations. It is a collective story waiting for our voices to express. That can only happen when you and I are willing to enter the emptiness, listening in the silence until we can understand how to create a future we can befriend.

I am wondering now, dear reader, about you. What are the courageous conversations you need to have with yourself, and how do you need to have them?

May we allow ourselves stillness so we can open our minds to ourselves, and spaciousness so we can allow a moment of rest when all thoughts fly above us like kites in a strong wind.

We all have islands of fear inside us, but we also all have continents of wisdom and truth. How do we find our way to them when we are not educated in the interior dimension? These inner landscapes hold the patterns of our passion and purpose. Without knowing how to journey there, our lives remain unlived.

CHAPTER 3

What Aileth Thee?

"We are now at a point in time when the ability to receive, utilize, store, transform and transmit data— the lowest cognitive form—has expanded literally beyond comprehension. Understanding and wisdom are largely forgotten as we struggle under an avalanche of data and information."
—DEE HOCK, *BIRTH OF THE CHAORDIC AGE*

STORIES ARE THE CURRENT OF MEANING, the river through which consciousness and culture move. This old, old story began some place back in the twelfth century with the search for the Holy Grail. There are as many versions of it as there are mysteries in the universe. This particular one tells of the struggle to breathe new life into a dying land, a dying people, and a dying soul:

In the center of space and time, there lived a king in a castle. His name was Arthur, and he had been mortally wounded. Though his heart still pumped blood, he never left his chamber, for he had fallen under an evil spell. He no longer cared a whit for the fortunes of his people or his lands. All of his kingdom lay fallow. Everyone's souls seemed to be suspended. The people went about their daily tasks lethargically, as if they were all in a trance of some kind. They had lost all sense of purpose.

The story now shifts to a cottage in the woods not far from the castle. A very naïve, fatherless young man named Parsifal had just come of age. While walking through the forest, he encountered a bevy of the king's knights riding along the road. He was so awestruck by their shining appearance that he immediately wished to become one such as they. Over the objections of his very strict mother, Herzelaide, he set off for the castle.

Parsifal was struck dumb, however, when he reached King Arthur's castle. Instead of the glorious Camelot he had expected, he found himself in the middle of a wasteland, where everything was sterile. He discovered that the king had been wounded in the groin, and had lost the power of re-generation. The King's courtiers, moving about listlessly, did nothing about the terrible situation that had befallen them.

Parsifal was given a horse and weapons so he could battle with a formidable knight who had bested all of Arthur's champions. Astonishingly, Parsifal won and took the armor of the fearsome foe. Some said it was mere luck, but the consensus was that the young man's innocence conferred a divine blessing on him.

Parsifal wanted desperately to help his king, but he, like everyone else, had no answers as to how to heal the wound. His mind was filled with questions, which flowed from the gift of his innocence, but he dammed them up, remembering his mother's constant injunction not to embarrass people by asking questions. And so Parsifal left the court on a quest for the Holy Grail.

The legend then relates how he ventured down many a blind path and false trail in his search, but finally, he glimpsed the Grail and, as a result, felt the King's pain in his own heart. On the first of May, he rode his magnificent white charger back to Arthur's castle. He rushed to his king, who was at Death's door. With compassion in his heart, he overcame his previous hesitancy and knelt beside his monarch. A question rose to his lips and spilled over as if it were wine.

"What aileth thee?" A blinding light flashed, and in an instant the spell was broken. The king's health was restored, the land and all its inhabitants were renewed. Arthur and the other members of the court turned to Parsifal and in honoring him, the King gave this toast, "If you falter, never forget, that verily every day holds the promise of a new redemption!"

Have you ever noticed how you tend to ask yourself the same questions every morning when you wake up? Where do I have to take the kids today? What's the market doing in Tokyo? Who do I have to call as soon as I get in the office? These questions are often the beginning of the tranquilizing spell we cast upon ourselves as we slip our feet into our comfy identity. We become who we've known ourselves to be—the harried Total Woman or the frenzied Entrepreneur. Perhaps the differences between us are really the differences in the questions we habitually ask ourselves. I asked a poet recently what was the first question she asked herself every morning. She replied without thinking, "Who was I before the alarm clock rang? Who was the stranger I was in my dreams?" A CEO, in response to the same question, told me before he got out of bed he asked himself, "What problems are waiting for me to solve today?" The two of them live very different lives.

Questions can be dangerous. They can take us right to the edge of what is known and comfortable. They can require tremendous courage to ask, because we know that new questions can lead to new ways of perceiving, and new perceptions can lead to new explorations of our world. Pick any question you have been avoiding asking yourself and you'll see what I mean. A question such as, "How did I make my work too small for me?" or "Is my spirit dying in my relationship?" or poet Mary Oliver's magnificently disturbing, "What is it that you want to do with the one, wild, precious thing called your life?"

Chaos and uncertainty often lead to the asking of new questions. Think about the former Soviet Union. The questions that are being asked there now would have been cause for being sent to Siberia a few years ago. The asking of new questions often leads us to the perilous, growing edge of our minds. That's because all new and original thought begins with a question, which leads to an exploration.

I spent most of my school years in a fervent dash for the perfect answer to every question. I accumulated information as if I were a hamster, stuffing it all in, ready to spit it out as soon as the appropriate question was asked. But cancer is a teacher that I can not impress with any answer. It takes me to a bridge where there are only questions that pry my heart open, as Parsifal's was to King Arthur's pain. These questions rescue me from the numbness of fear and cynicism, and return me to a second innocence where, like Parsifal, I can ask myself, "What aileth thee?" Questions such as this make it possible for emptiness to open, so we can listen to the truth about what we really feel. Only then can we say to our wounds, "Even here, love can grow." When this happens, as with King Arthur and his court, we can awaken.

Can we embrace the unanswered? Can we live in the mystery? What is required of us is to remember what we knew as young children in our most fertile learning state. Spend ten minutes with a three-year-old and you'll see what I mean. If you read the diaries or journals of some of the greatest minds in our times—Albert Einstein, Virginia Woolf, Aldous Huxley, Howard Thurman, to name a few—you'll discover that throughout their lives, they ask wide and open questions of themselves, spending years pondering them, playing in them as a child does in a swing.

Certain kinds of questions evoke the purpose and passion that are always alive in our intuitive minds. They cause us to step back from seeing the tiny details and dots of our daily existence, and help us perceive the whole picture, the deeper meaning of who we are and why we are alive. They take us on the journey from emptiness to openness to wonder to imagination to wisdom. Have you ever had a question that was really puzzling you and then you stepped into a shower, forgetting about it? But as you stepped out and toweled off, you saw it in a whole new way, Pop goes the riddle! I call what has happened while you were in the shower "mental metabolism," which refers to the mind's ability to intuitively digest our question without our being consciously aware of it.

The brain has both analytic and intuitive ways of processing information. They are meant to work hand in hand, but usually end up in an arm wrestle. If we analyze only as we have been taught to do in most schools, snapping at the first answer that comes along, then judging it good or bad, right or wrong, the shy intuitive mind, not unlike a prairie dog, runs for cover. Analysis, when improperly done, causes paralysis. It creates a world "out there," of which we are only spectators and in which we do not live. This is commonly called objectivity.

If, on the other hand, the analytic mind asks open questions of discernment—"I wonder how this could work. . . . What would it look like if this were really possible? . . ." the intuitive mind begins to explore many possibilities, weaving its way through the trees until it has a sense of the whole forest and its meaning in nature's scheme of things. Pop!

This wandering and wondering are not useful when one is dealing with issues such as the computation of income taxes. But the exploration of purpose and passion requires us to uncover patterns and understand the relatedness between things, and then synthesize them into a new whole. This is the terrain of intuitive processing. Personal truth can not be found in either analytic thinking or intuitive thinking alone. It can only be uncovered in an open inquiry between them.

After two weeks of being on retreat, I was in danger of moving from "empty" to a state of stupor. One Sunday morning, I noticed how many questions were flying around the rooftops of my mind. So I dumped every one I could find onto a very large piece of paper. The first thirty were neither open nor evocative. They were the usual ones I had been waking up with for months. I kept going, insisting I not stop until I had come up with one hundred questions, not trying to be clever or philosophical. What was important was that they were questions that were true for me. Questions thirty through sixty began to reveal themes: relationships, for example. I kept going, deeper and darker, until it felt as if the last questions were right at the axis of my existence and exploring them could mean shifting my entire gravitational field. When I was finished, a pale suspended emptiness moved in me, pulling free the tight-gathered knot of worries the past months had spun. My mind felt clean, like a wind had blown through.

I condensed the questions down until I had the ones that were compelling enough to evoke my mind into wonder. Each of those became a polestar which, one after the other, I asked myself every morning upon waking until it was no longer evocative to me. I just sat with it, letting my mind wander, bringing it back to the question, wander, wonder, wander.

"How do I live divided no more?" was my focal point in this way for two weeks. After a short time of noticing where my mind would fly when I asked it, I'd draw whatever image came to me, then journal the sensations I felt in my body and the stories that arose. I used it as a rhythm setter for snowshoeing, one word for each step and breath, and I wrote it down in a notebook before I went to sleep, delivering it to my dreaming mind.

There was a time I really wanted company in this questioning process, without simultaneously breaking my solitude. So I wrote a letter to thirty-five friends, asking them to join me in this exploration by sending me the evocative question that was currently the axis of their life. Thirty-two responded. I slipped these, one by one, under the glass top of my desk as companions on the quest. Here are some of them:

"What do I have to believe about death to fully celebrate life?"—Juliy

"How can I expand my compassion into proactive passion?" —Lisa

"What is the imagining of life that I am the expression of?" —Glenna

"What's down this road, and who is doing what to whom?" —Riki

"Where does my gift end?" —Wendy

"What aspects of myself do I assume need changing and why?" —Nancy

"If the coping skills I've developed to achieve safety were to suddenly drop away, how would I live?" —Dale

"Where am I going? Do I really want to go there? Is there anything I can do about it?" —Justine

"Will I have the guts?" —LeeAnn

"Where will I be and will I be able to feel when I'm finally free?" —Stef

"What is my theory about how change happens?" —Beth

"When I am working, what do I think I am working on?"
—Glennifer

"How do I co-create the conditions in which all people and other living things flourish, bequeathing a resilient and compassionate community?" —Bea

"How can I be my most true self?" —Marjean

"Is what I'm choosing full of life and energy?" —Judy

The questions that were distilled from my one hundred and the stories, images, and dreams that emerged as I wandered with them form and inform this book. Without them, its contents would be like a body without bones.

I'm curious now, dear reader, what question you would have sent to me and what question would evoke the deepest wonder in your mind at this time in your life. I offer you two right now as companions on the journey:

What (people, places, events, situations) deplete your energy? What generates energy for you?

What is it too soon for, too late for, just the right time for?

May we all find the courage we need to ask ourselves the questions that will free our minds and strengthen our souls.

Retreating into oneself to find purpose can be like straddling a boat leaving the dock, pulled in opposite directions by the intense desire of the mind for human involvement and the equally intense need of the soul for its own company. In the sheer immensity of solitude, when one can no longer draw energy from external sources, we come to see how much of what we habitually call meaningful purpose is merely the evasion of sitting still and meeting what is most difficult for us to receive with compassion—our own pain.

CHAPTER 4

As Is

"Even here, in the silence of this room, I am not alone. This silence is alive with the unfolding of other lives and with the turning and movement of the Earth. I began to sense my connection to the world's pain and my part in healing it. I realized that my transformation of pain into love was an act of service for humankind. By embracing my existence, I could bring courage to others to face their own pain and to acknowledge what it had to teach them."

—YAEL BETHEIM, *THE UNHEALED LIFE*

WHEN I WAS IN THE HOSPITAL BEING TREATED FOR CANCER, the one person whose presence I welcomed was a Jamaican woman who came to sweep the floors with a large pushbroom. Of the fifty or so people that made contact with me in any given day, she was the only one who wasn't trying to change me, the only one who didn't stick things in, take things out, or ask stupid questions. For a few minutes each night, she rested her broom against the wall and sank her immense body into the turquoise plastic chair in my room. All I could hear was the sound of her breath going in and out, in and out. It was comforting in a strange and simple way. My own breathing settled down, following hers, and became calm.

One night she reached out and put her hand on my foot. I'm usually not comfortable with casual touch, but her hand felt so natural being there, on one of the few places in my body that didn't hurt. I could have sworn she was saying two words with each breath, one on the inhale, one on the exhale: "As . . . is . . . As . . . is . . ."

On her next visit, she looked at me. No evaluation in her buttery brown eyes, no trying to figure me out. She just looked and saw me, completely. Then she said quietly, firmly, "You're more than the sickness in that body." The words seem larger and fuller than herself. I was pretty doped up, so I wasn't sure I understood her correctly, but my mind was just too thick to ask questions at that point.

I kept mumbling those words to myself throughout the following day, "I'm more than the sickness in this body." I remembered her voice clearly. It was rich, full, like maple syrup in the spring. It carried me breathing deeply into a fog of silence.

When the nurse came with my shot of morphine the next night, I refused it. I wanted to find out if my nighttime angel was real or a drugged hallucination. An hour or so later, I heard the sound of her broom brushing against the marble hall floors. Her body filled up the whole doorway, and cast a long shadow on the floor of my room. She sank into the chair. The pain I was feeling was intense. She breathed loudly, then, after a few minutes, said, "You're not the pain in that body. It's there, but you're more than that pain."

I reached out for her hand. It was cool and dry. I knew she wouldn't let go. She continued, "You're not the fear in that body. You're more than that fear. Float on it. Float above it. You're more than that pain." I began to breathe a little deeper as I did when I wanted to float in a lake. I remembered floating in Lake George when I was five, floating in the Atlantic Ocean at Coney Island when I was seven, floating in the Indian Ocean off the coast of Africa when I was twenty-eight. Without any instructions from me, this Jamaican angel had led me to a source of comfort that was wider and deeper than pain or fear.

It's been almost three decades since I've seen this woman with the broom. I spent months trying to find her when I got out of the hospital, but to no avail. No one could even remember her name, but she touched my soul with her compassionate presence and her fingerprints are there still.

The lessons I learned from the Jamaican angel have stayed in my mind and grown in my heart like seedlings taking root in good soil. They have continued growing during my healing process, sent out runners when I needed them, and here, alone on this barren mountaintop, like a prolific strawberry patch, they bear fruit.

The point of spending time in solitude is stripping oneself bare to discover what is at one's essence. An Aikido teacher once told me, "Calm your mind until it is like water settling. The waves will disappear and the surface will be smooth as glass." What he forgot to tell me is that when the water of your mind calms down, it doesn't feel anything like peace. Because all you have to do is bend over and look down. What you find is all the junk settled on the bottom where you can see it clearly. If, instead, you keep the water stirred up, everything hides in the murk where you don't have to respond to it at all.

What I was taught, and perhaps you were as well, is to disconnect from "the junk"—the pain or fear—so I wouldn't feel it. Which is not how the Jamaican angel responded to me. What I learned from her was a different way to relate to what is difficult: first create spaciousness inside myself by remembering that I am more than my pain, more than my confusion, more than my fear, more than the stories I can tell myself about those feelings. Then, I can connect with what hurts. This is how I first discovered that compassion is the skillful way to respond to pain and difficulty. It is what makes it possible to open to what is occurring instead of shutting it out or walling off against it.

From another great teacher in my life, Victor Frankl, author of *Man's Search for Meaning*, I learned about personal freedom. When he was in a concentration camp, he discovered that each of us is always free to choose what meaning we attach to any given experience, internal or external. Even the Nazi prison guards, torture, and starvation could not take away Frankl's belief that he was going through all of that because he was supposed to teach the world about creating peace when the war was over. Many others in his situation thought of themselves as victims. But Frankl refused that story, choosing instead to believe he could be a victor.

These lessons from two great souls are, for me, the essence of skillful befriending.

Someone once told me the art of success is using what you're good at to overcome the challenges that life brings you. Everyone's good at something. My sister is good at bringing beauty into the world, Andy's good at translating the joy he feels at being alive in a body into music. I've always been good at befriending people. I've made it my profession, first as a teacher, then a psychotherapist, now a thinking partner to organizations. It's also been the way I've related to my disease. When cancer first came into my life, people all around me treated it as the enemy. I was told I had to join the medical team and we'd fight together to defeat it. This was the wrong thing to say to someone who was the last one to be picked for any team. I was much happier sitting on the sidelines and encouraging the other players. I was totally unskilled at defeating anything. So I secretly went my own way and decided that I was free to choose the meaning of the healing experience. I decided I would develop a friendly relationship with the cancer, which was something I was good at.

Successful as I have been at befriending others and a major disease, coming to these mountains by myself requires a whole new level and kind of befriending. I am having to learn to relate to those inner demons of doubt and guardians at the gate to my soul, who have been doing their best for years to keep me from exposing myself, my shadows, my failures, my successes; to prevent me from offending my sister, dead relatives, son, husband, and anyone who has ever been affiliated with me in any way.

Befriending myself seems to be about opening my heart as a homeless shelter for all the destitute and prostituted aspects of my being that I have been running from for years without even knowing that that's what I have been doing. It seems to mean telling myself the complete truth about everything, without telling myself stories about the horrible things that will happen as a result, the hatred that will be incurred, for example, if I don't phone back all the people that call me. It means noticing the energy of my experience without ignoring, repressing, or acting on it. Befriending myself means becoming a refuge to and for myself so that I can be one for others. Ultimately, it means finding the courage to give myself the kind of presence and attention I have been giving to others for years. Not courage as in blood and guts, but as in rooting in one's darkness and allowing a sense of meaning to grow there.

Taming a mind like mine to let go of all of the horror stories for a moment or two is quite simple, but it's not so easy. It's like training Shaka, my Golden Retriever, to drop the socks she picks up in her mouth whenever she gets nervous or scared: "Drop it, Shaka, lie down. Good dog, now stay. . . . Shaka, I said drop it." As I train her, I train myself to drop the stories I tell myself about me and the world, to drop the secure and all-too-comfortable small masks I wear to know who I am. I think Shaka learns more quickly than I do.

This morning, my "training session" went something like this:

Just sit down now and let the tears come. The reason they are welling doesn't matter. Just stay with the sensations of the feeling itself, the energy.

That's right. Drop it. Just stay with the sensations of the fear of the feeling. Drop it.

That's right, just stay with the sensations caused by judging the fear of the feeling and saying I'm a coward. Drop it.

Just stay with the sensations in my chest and belly and throat, including the sadness about the judging. Drop it.

Just stay with the feeling of nakedness and fragility. It doesn't need to wear a story, it wants to feel its own skin. The feeling is more alive than the stories. The feeling is the energy moving through you. The tears are your soul washing itself clean. Drop it. . . .

As I learn to "drop" the stories and be present with what I actually experience, I have flashes of realizing that every person who has ever lived probably felt the very same thing I am feeling at some point in their lives. This seems like the first wedge of freedom in my mind. It leaves a kind of glimmering tenderness around the edges of my heart toward all of us who share the condition known as humankind.

Anne Morrow Lindbergh wrote, "When one is a stranger to oneself, then one is estranged from others. . . . Only when one is connected to one's core is one truly connected to others." Perhaps befriending the energy we meet when we turn inward to reconnect with our true selves can ultimately become a steppingstone for understanding the experience of other people. Perhaps relating in this way can give our pain meaning instead of having it spin off into words and actions or repressions that cause so much anguish. Perhaps, when you allow your heart and mind to pay attention to each other in a clean way, when silence becomes a loom, the still, small voice that is your soul can reweave the pattern that is the purpose of how you are living your life.

I am wondering now, dear reader, where your mind goes when you sit or walk in a stilled moment under an immense sky. Who is the "you" that notices those thoughts?

May our quest for purpose be compassionate. May it be like a pebble dropped into the middle of this moment. May it ripple out over the surface of the space between us.

II

Living On Fire: Landscapes of the Heart

"From the seed grows a root, then a sprout; from
the sprout, the seedling leaves; from the leaves, the
stem; around the stem, the branches; at the top,
the flower.... We cannot say that the seed causes
the growth, nor that the soil does. We can say that
the potentialities for growth lies within the seed,
in mysterious life forces, which, when properly
fostered, take on certain forms."

—M. C. RICHARDS, *CENTERING: IN POTTERY,
POETRY AND THE PERSON*

Two months wrapped in memory and meditation.
I am sitting in what was my mother's chair at what
was my father's desk on a pillow I bought for
myself that says, "Welcome to Our Cabin." When
I look out the windows to the right or to the left, all I can see
is the swirl and swoop of snow, and the shadows of big old

spruce trees, a circle of silent sentinels. I am sitting in the middle of a blizzard and the sky overhead, like God's eye winking, is bright blue. A half-hour ago, big gray buffalo stormclouds completely engulfed the mountains. Such a vast expanse, wide enough to hold several weathers all at the same time. This sky is teaching me about what my mind can be and do.

It's past one in the afternoon and I haven't eaten yet. I'm not hungry. I'm waiting for a signal from the inside. My body must know when it needs food. I'm breaking so many habitual rules and instructions that lodged themselves in my brain decades ago. I've been peeling away the rigid beliefs and attitudes, rhythms and reasons that keep me numb and closed in as if they were cornhusks.

To explore what it would mean to live fully, sensually alive and passionately on purpose, I have to drop my preconceived ideas of who and what I am. It is as if the salt of years is running free from me. Like so many of us, my head has been stuffed full of knowledge, but something in me is still starving. So here, I seek to empty it of the stories, explanations, and interpretations I am clutching in the fist of my mind. When did it get so tightly closed that it became numb? And what was it holding onto anyway? I want it free. I want my heart and soul free. Free of and free from. Free of struggle, free from doubt in the canyons of my bones, free from running from the truth of knowing that something has been missing.

Unclutching, emptying, opening, then wondering, as if I am releasing a small bird. I look at my hands. The left one shows a pattern of four arteries like a river, while the right one is like a web. They are my hands and I haven't really noticed them since I was a child. Where do the images come from that they have been drawing on the empty pages of my journal? Where do my dreams come from, now that I am eager to give attention to their mystery? And where do the stories come from that gush forth onto the page even when there's no one to entertain? Something is happening. Questions float in the night like moths.

Wondering. What am I reaching for? What is the urge that calls me beyond the familiar into unexplored territory? What is smoldering inside me? My passion is missing. Where is my passion? Has it unraveled from wear and tear?

I found a paper wasp's nest hanging abandoned from an aspen branch in the woods yesterday, an empty husk. It spoke to me: *I am gray and dry now. My round womb-like husk is layered with many thin but tough sheets of paper. I hide a honeycomb that once was filled with a hive of life. They swarmed in me, all around me. They were a colony with individual directions and intentions, but they were also one larger self. Now they are gone. I am hollow. I have served my purpose. I am a reminder of all the life that was born in me and moved through me. I hang here waiting to be found, perhaps to be cherished for all I have contained and been.*

It haunts me. Is it a mirror for my passion? By *passion* I don't mean sex or desire. I don't mean what happens to you when you wear Obsession, drive a Porsche Carrera, weigh ninety-six pounds, and are lusted after by someone with a deep cleft in his chin. I mean the natural life energy that exists inside each of us, urging growth. A deep and natural pulse that tells us to live from the inside out, to reach in and reach out for all that is possible to know, to contribute, and to receive. I may have lost the feeling of it right now, but I am beginning to think passion exists in the relationship between things, between the self and the rest of life, between forces in opposition to each other, between polarities and paradoxes, between and beyond the river of either/or that seems to divide so much of our world.

Norman Cousins wrote that recovery from a major illness correlates with a passionate involvement in life. Well, I thought I was passionately involved, but it seems I was really just purposelessly busy, telling myself all the time that what I was doing was urgent. How do I find a better place from which to live my life? And speaking of better places, why did I choose this frozen, icy environment to write about passion, this dark and virgin territory to find a path and a little light? Why not Jamaica, or Hawaii? Why not cascades of fuchsia and apricot bougainvillea, piña coladas and mango salsa, my body naked and baking, my hips swiveling to a lush lambada beat?

Unfortunately, this is exactly the right external topography to match my inner state of being. I'm sure there are fierce yearnings of heart and soul under the smooth, flat surface of the frenetic life I was living. But for now, all I feel is empty. Under a vast and constantly changing sky, I'm surrounded by a natural dormancy where passion's spark is buried and has to be searched for.

I've found my way into this dormancy by asking questions that probably only God can answer, impossible questions that flap in my mind like sheets in the wind: How do we reclaim our lost fire? How do we remember that our love really does matter? How do we retrieve our leaking souls?

Anything capable of decay is also capable of regeneration. Passion is a given when we are young. As children we burn with it, unless it gets smothered or beaten out of us. But as adults, it becomes so elusive, as if there were thin ribbony veils of music playing someplace just beyond our everyday hearing, pale and near-transparent. How do we evoke the untamable in ourselves, the part that dreams and imagines beyond what is known? How do we open fully to what life brings us, letting it lift us and carry us?

I stumble forward in a dim light, finding my way to the vitality that is passion one step at a time. I come to four doors, closed at my heart: rage, denial, inertia, and loss. I believe most of us were taught to slam these shut, turn our backs, and lean up against them in fear. But I also believe that on the other side of these doors are passageways to our brightest fire, the choice to live fully awake and alive.

*How do we walk through the door of rage to find our passion,
which is what we fear and yearn for most? We fear it
because it promises to be spontaneous, out of our control,
beyond our reasonable and known selves. We yearn for it
because passion has color, dimension, pulse. It reveals the
back side of our hearts, our blessed wildness.*

CHAPTER 5

Catching Fire

"This is the charged, the dangerous moment, when
everything must be re-examined, must be made new,
when nothing at all can be taken for granted."
—JAMES BALDWIN

BEAR WITH ME. I'VE BEEN THINKING OF MY SOUL RECENTLY. Soul
thinking won't follow a straight line.

I have been living in a war zone for fifty-seven years. That's as
good a place to begin as any.

As a young girl, I was addicted to *Wonder Woman* comic books. My mother kept buying me *Little Lulu* and *Archie & Veronica*. I traded them all for *Wonder Woman*, my one and only heroine. This was before I learned that Emma Goldman, the radical revolutionary spirit of the '30s, was my great-aunt.

Our family was divided into two sides: the Red-Communist, Radical, on-my-father's-side, whom we didn't speak about; and the White-Capitalist, American, Neutral, on-my-mother's-side.

My father's view of the world was also bifurcated—there were good guys and there were bad guys. Since I used to love to watch Roy Rogers and Gene Autry on television, I assumed the good guys all wore white hats and the bad guys all wore red hats, but since we only had black and white television back then I had to imagine the red hats. Every night he'd come home from work with a new chapter in the epic story of how Brian Knight and Ray Maxwell (who both wore red hats) tried to pull my father down as he scrambled up the ladder of success (wearing his white felt fedora). Of course they were anti-Semites, Nazis, bad guys, but I didn't have to worry because Dwight David Eisenhower was a good guy, even though he wasn't Jewish, and he'd help my father out.

When he finally got to the top of that ladder, having worked his way up from a Hell's Kitchen street fighter to the president of one of America's major corporations, we moved to Chicago. At first we lived in a very fancy apartment on Lake Shore Drive, which my mother loved. But my father's peasant blood wanted to be the first generation of his family to own land. So we went searching in the suburbs, and found a white colonial mansion, complete with oak trees and rolling green lawns, right next to the

Washover Country Club. The real estate agent was unctuous, oily, supercilious, like Uriah Heep in *David Copperfield*. His smile never stopped as my father began to sign the sales agreement, and he turned to my mother, casually asking, "By the way, Ma'am, which church do you go to?"

Now it wasn't that my mother was timid. She just got very confused in situations when she didn't know how to be neutral. She cleared her throat and got her Jew-in-the-concentration-camp look, and turned to my father.

His response was immediate. "We don't go to church. We go to temple. We're Jewish." As the real estate agent pulled the paper out from my father's hands, he mumbled, "It's not me you understand. Some of my best friends are Hebrews, but the neighbors...."

What I remember next was my father's jaw getting Dick Tracy-sharp, and his fist in the bad guy's face, with a comic book bubble above reading, "KAPOW!"

This was not the first time I had experienced my father's rage. It usually exploded in totally unpredictable ways. The problem was that you never could tell who was one of the bad guys, or when my father's struggle against wrong would include my mother or sister or me. We all developed our own ways of avoiding or diverting his fire. My mother turned to ice and ignored it. My sister became Perfect, never doing anything wrong, and I became a storyteller, capable of rearranging any events to give them the most effective meaning possible.

As we left the real estate office and drove past the country club, I noticed a large sign lettered in gold gothic print. Before I tell you what it said, I better let you in on the family secret. My father couldn't read. No one knew except my mother and me. How he managed to get where he got to as a functional illiterate is another story, but suffice it to say that she and I covered for him. We'd read things into a reel-to-reel tape recorder, which he'd listen to in the dark of night. He had total auditory recall, and he could pretend really well when he needed to.

So back to the sign. It read:

**Washover Country Club
Restricted
*No Jews or Dogs Allowed***

My mother gasped in the back seat. My father asked what was the matter. Before she could respond and before he could put his fist in someone else's face, maybe mine, I said, "Oh nothing Daddy. That sign says,

**Washover Country Club
Restricted? No!
Jews or Dogs Allowed!"**

From the time I was five until I was fourteen, my mother insisted I go to summer camp so she and my father could have a vacation. I hated every second of camp. Especially the color wars. There was always a color war. On the morning teams were picked, I would hide under a boat dock, reading *Wonder Woman* comic books. I considered balls, nets, rackets, bats, and gloves instruments of torture, and stayed as far from them as was humanly possible. I was, therefore, always chosen last to be on any team.

Color war—red and white divided. Three years ago I was

diagnosed with a form of leukemia that caused my blood cells to be divided. The way I understand it is that the red blood cells kept collapsing and couldn't hold oxygen very well. The white ones, which are supposed to zip around like little Electrolux vacuum cleaners, were few and far between and schlepped instead of zipped, leaving me exhausted and unprotected from what had become a gray and dangerous world. The red and white cells were not in communication with each other. One does not have to be a Grand Symbologist to understand that at a cellular level, like it or not, I was still living a color war.

I had two very interesting dreams the night I came to this cabin to rekindle my passion for living. In the first, there was a young girl, maybe eight or nine years old. She was wearing red shorts and a white tee shirt. Her hair was pulled into two bunches, one with a white ribbon, one with a red. She was tap dancing in a concentration camp. All around her, gaunt bodies lay on pallets, but as far as she was concerned she could have been on stage at Rockefeller Center.

When I pulled up our old rocking chair in front of the fire to write the dream down in my journal, I immediately realized that I was here to camp out, to concentrate on the questions that really mattered, to tap in curious exploration between all the apparent contradictions and confusions in my life until I could dance back and forth and find my own integrity.

In the second dream, I stood at the front door to a house. I banged on a brass knocker in the shape of a lion's head. My father opened the door. He was old, shrunken, his watery blue eyes reflecting nothing, as he had been in the last years of his life. Alzheimer's left the raging corporate leader of thousands absent of any presence. I hugged him but he pulled back and slammed the door in my face. The dream recurred for many nights. And then it changed. This time I rapped on the door, but the person who opened it was not my father. It was me ... an older me, but equally vacant and empty as he had been. It seemed at first that she was about to slam the door as he had, but then she breathed, reached out over the threshold, and laughed as she said, "I don't know who the hell you are, but come on in anyway!"

How do I parent my passion? I always thought I had to choose between being out of control and full of aggression like my father was, fighting against the bad guys who could be blamed for all the suffering in the world, or totally in control, a victim who disappeared behind her own ice walls and ignored everything, the way my mother did. Where does passion live in these two choices?

Next to my desk on a little gold easel sits a bright red *Wonder Woman* comic book that my son and daughter-in-love bought me for Xmas. It is dated January 12, 1964, and on its cover, there she is, complete with bullet-proof bracelets, red lace-up high-heeled boots, and, of course, a golden rope at her waist. She is lifting a tree out of the ground and using it to stave off a fire-breathing Tyrannosaurus Rex. In the bubble above her head, she says, "Great Hera! If this is the first obstacle in my mission, what will the others be like?!" She causes me to wonder how I can swing back and forth in the widest mind I can find, to create reconciliation between fire and ice.

My father discussed options by saying, "On the one hand ... But on the other hand...." And then he'd decide which one was right and which one was wrong. Even then, I knew God gave us two hands and two arms, and two eyes and two halves of our brains to work together. We walk one foot in front of the other, hear both sides of a story. There is no division in nature, and we are natural creatures, seeking the birthright of our own integrity. When and why did we create the abyss between ideas and feelings, logic and art, science and religion, work and play, heart and mind?

I begin to notice my breath the way I learned from Dr. Milton Erickson. He had sparking blue eyes like my father, but lived much of his life in a wheelchair. That must have been where he learned to maneuver so well between forces in opposition. He taught about psychotherapy and hypnotherapy. One day he said, "People will come to you wearing masks. We all wear masks. They will come and show you the outside of the mask, but after a while, they'll show you the other side, the concave side." Then he paused. I leaned in and waited. Finally, he winked and continued, "Your real job is to help them create a relationship between those two sides of the mask. And you can best do that...." Another pause, more leaning, "by giving your attention to the great wisdom of your breath."

As I remembered this, the past, the present, and the future melted together. Instead of feeling pulled apart or trapped between all the polarities, I noticed the relationship between my in-breath and my out-breath, how effortlessly they flowed one into the other, a continuous loop of letting go of the stale and old, letting in the fresh and new. What was old that I had to let go of?

Words swirled in the air like fine dust. "Rage is passion without choice." They settled into a memory that clogged my heart. I was five; my father carried me into the ocean at Coney Island. He put one large, square hand on my back, the other on my neck, and told me to lie back. Without question, I relaxed completely into the support of those hands. Those hands would protect my five-year-old body. Those hands were more powerful than the might of the entire Atlantic Ocean.

How could those hands that supported me as I rose and fell in the salty sea rise and fall with a belt that same night? How could they beat my tender body until I disappeared into blackness? How could the voice that crooned, "Ah, ah, baby," pierce the darkness with the words, "Now look at what you made me do. I tried not to, but you made me so mad all I could see was red. I didn't mean to do it. I didn't do it on purpose. I tried, but I just lost control. Now you be a good girl and I'll never have to do it again." But those hands couldn't keep the promise of those words. They beat me again and again, because I could never be that good.

How do I learn to father my passion in a different way? He is long dead now. I know I can forgive the man and never have to forgive his actions. Some time ago, I heard myself say, "I have tried to forgive him for years, but I get so mad when I even think about what he did, I want to smash him." And then a key began to turn in my mind. We were in the same place. The twisted seed of passion, rage, lived in me as well. Unless I open the door of my heart to it, unless I find new ways to relate and respond to it, I will never have full access to the vitality that is hidden at its core.

The man who raped me in rage, and the men I slept with to "take the war out of them," as author Deena Metzger says, are also long gone from my life. I came through all of that. I made it.

Rage is passion without choice. We become its involuntary passengers. But what is the point at which I still have choice? What are the choices that are mine to make? I buried certain beliefs with my father, certain stories he told himself and assumptions he made that led him to violence. In my mind, I threw into his coffin the belief that rage just happens to you, that something on the outside can make you feel that way, make you do what you do not choose to do. I also buried the assumption that we can "control" ourselves and the world enough to never feel anger or rage.

It was as if one of the unlimited aches in the world had finally mended in me, and a kind of brightness flooded out. What my father saw as the division between "either" and "or," I now see as a gap waiting to be bridged. What if, in times of conflict or anger, we threw every story we tell ourselves about who is right and who is wrong, who is bad and who is good into that gap? What if you were to stand at the edge of that precipice as your fire rises and do nothing but notice the sensations your body? What if I were to stand there long enough to notice my breath rise and fall, long enough to notice the space before and after inspiration and do nothing more than ask myself, "What do I really need now?"

When David was an infant and on the threshold of gaining a new skill—walking, speaking, leaping—he would sometimes scream and shake in complete frustration and rage. I couldn't reason with him. I felt totally helpless. All I could do was follow what seemed most natural: hold him, walk with him, rock him, and murmur, "Ah, ah, baby," wondering what he needed. In minutes (that sometimes felt like years), his body softened, and he'd nestle his wet cheek into my neck. Then he'd wiggle down, ready to try again.

Can we father our own fire this way? Can we drop all stories and explanations of why we feel what we feel and whose fault it is and what we should do about it? Instead of constricting or lashing out, can we expand the space inside ourselves so we can just notice the sensations in our bodies and swing from Wonder Woman's golden rope into the unknown? Do we dare to feel the white heat of our hearts as a prayer? Can we risk knowing what is smoldering inside of us?

We all are storytellers. We all take a bit of experience and stretch it into a story that makes meaning from it and determines what actions we take or repress. My back is twingeing as I sit here. Sensation. The data of my current experience. Then comes a story. "I must have pulled a muscle skiing." Or, "I probably have a tumor on my spine." Or, "It's my husband Andy's fault for not letting me sleep on the side of the bed I wanted to last night." If I'm not aware I am creating these stories, I have no choice. Once, however, we begin to give attention to the space between impulse and action, to the "sizzle point" of fire rising, we can notice how we shape our experience.

I think of all the people since the beginning of time who have felt the energy we call rage. Because none of us knows how to befriend this energy, it spins off into words or actions that cause so much abuse and suffering. When I remember that all rage is like my rage, I can find the comfort of a shared humanity.

I wish I could say this lesson could be readily mastered. Don't you? But it seems to be more of a practice, like any other art form, that comes knocking with a forceful fist on our doorstep many times a day. How will we choose to respond each time we open the door?

My grandmother used to wash her front stoop so when people took the first step into her house, it would be clean. Well, on last New Year's Day, the much-awaited crossing of the threshold into the new millennium, I made a muddy mess on mine. I had a horrendous fight with Andy. I can't remember the reason. We hadn't even finished our morning orange juice before I had decided that he was trying to get me. I think he forgot to say Happy New Year and I decided he was a heavy, depressed dude. The day before I was enchanted with how grounded he was, but on this day he had magically transformed into the Dark Demon of Despair, with whom I could no longer spend another minute. I wanted to kill him. Really. I was on fire. And then, instead of lashing out, I sat down and fell into the loyal arms of my journal. Without thinking, my hand wrote, "Seeing red, I am unable to care." That's all it took. I dropped the pen and just began to breathe. Inoutinout. Space. In and out. Space. In space out space. The fire turned to embers and my heart creaked open on its rusty hinges. I imagined myself in so much pain. Each breath, I inhaled her pain, and exhaled caring. "Ah, ah, baby. "

There was no magical transformation. I just found ground again. Seven or eight times that day . . . well, maybe ten or eleven, I began to sob, for no reason that I could discern: the soup boiled over, Andy sneezed, the dog wagged her tail, David hugged me and said, "Happy New Year."

Each time I did the same thing: I climbed back in my body, and noticed the sensations themselves, refusing any story my mind crafted. I breathed in the pain of my fragility, breathed out compassion and mercy. Then I began to breathe in what I saw as Andy's dreaded darkness and breathe out to him light and spaciousness. Finally, I drew an image in my journal of what I was actually experiencing. It looked like a pale and puny white shoot pushing its fragile nose against a brown, sodden leaf mulch in the early spring. I realized how those thick, dark, wet leaves had been protecting it until there was enough light and warmth for it to reach for the sun. Looking at the drawing, I understood that both of those energies were in me. The heavy brownness was how I kept my rage buried. The tender white shoots were from healthy new seeds trying to emerge.

The rut of rage opened into a river of passion that runs through my veins and arteries, through my red blood cells and white blood cells. I imagine it running clear and clean from my father, through me to my son. I imagine it flowing out to all of us who search for reconciliation with our fire.

And it leads me to wonder, dear reader, from whom did you learn about fire? Was there someone who passed a twisted seed of rage to you? If you were to transform it, what shape would the energy take and how could it burn in a wholesome way for you and the rest of the world?

May all of us who want to transform rage find the courage to imagine it becoming an outrageous possibility of sanity that lies deeper than habit or thought.

How do we walk through the door of denial to evoke and strengthen passion? My mother's death taught me that this requires melting the frozen ice floes that block us from nurturing what we truly love. Rather than trying to be secure by merely keeping ourselves alive, the relevant focus of our passion needs to become taking the necessary risks so that the thing in us that loves, and the things it loves, stay alive and are passed on.

CHAPTER 6

Falling Free

"Let yourself be silently drawn by the stronger pull of
what you really love."
—RUMI

MY PARENTS DIDN'T PLAY MUCH. Like most of their friends, they worked hard and saved up money so they would be safe. Being safe was the single most important motivation of their lives. I thought being safe would happen when we could finally live in a house of our own. But they bought a house, and it still wasn't safe because my sister and I had to go to college. No one in either of my parents' families had ever gone to college. But even when both of us finished school, it wouldn't be safe until they retired. When they finally sold their house and went to Florida, it was time to be safe. My father would play golf. They could both swim in the ocean and go out to restaurants every night. They moved into an apartment building with a security guard who made sure no one dangerous got in. I was certain this would make my insecure mother happy.

My mother told me she had never spent a day in her life when she wasn't afraid. She was insecure about being alone in their apartment because the people who came to fix things might be dangerous. She went to the intensive care ward with congestive heart failure. Heart failure. Intensive care. Then she developed arthritis and had to push herself behind a walker, which was really a little metal set of walls.

My father's best friend, who was eighty-two, accused him on the golf course of lying about his score on the sixteenth hole. My father punched him in the nose, and they never spoke to each other again. My mother decided the golf course was too dangerous. Then she read about someone drowning in the ocean off of West Palm Beach, so they stopped going there too. Less than a year after they moved, they were living almost exclusively behind walls that kept closing in on them, until finally they barricaded their hearts and minds. But the walls didn't keep the danger or the pain out. They just drove it deeper.

No one would have called my mother passionate. My father was the passionate one. Everyone who knew him would have used the word *passionate* in the first five words. My mother was neat. Friendly. Others would have described her as kind and caring. She was also resentful, and a bit of a martyr. But no one would have said that. Except me.

She was so neat that she never taught me the words for bodily functions. We just ignored them. We ignored a lot of things. Death, for instance.

"Just don't think about it, Dawna. Pretend it's not there. What good will thinking about it do? You can't control it, so ignore it."

My mother was right about a lot of things. She did a lot of things well. She spent most of her life tending to others, writing birthday and sympathy cards in a scrawling, skinny left-hand script. She loved flowers and people. In the photograph I treasure most of her, she is standing on the long passageway outside her apartment, one arm around a bunch of red roses and the other around me. She is clutching both of us so tightly that I am crushed into smiling. She gave me love as seed. She gave me love of others as blossom.

A few weeks before she died, she told me she had always been afraid of losing me because she thought I was smarter than she was. She had never said that before, but somehow I must have known. I remember "dumbing myself down"—erasing the right answers on tests and putting in wrong ones on purpose, editing words in my mouth that might sound too smart. I wanted to stay attached to her. I wanted to keep having an inferiority complex, just like she said we both had. So we wrapped our inferior umbilical cords around each other's hearts, and I spent decades trying not to be too brave or too smart so I could stay attached to her.

Now she whispers in my ear not to tell how she died. "It wasn't right. It wasn't nice. I don't want people to think of me in that way."

There were things she was wrong about. I do have to tell you how she died. She died on the floor in the middle of the night crawling to the bathroom, alone. Nothing my sister and I did could prevent that. The night nurse was asleep on the couch in the living room. The button to call her was clipped to the sheet next to my mother's shaky left hand in the hospital bed we rented. Maybe she was in a daze and forgot to push it, maybe she was too weak, or more likely, she fell on her way to the bathroom, refusing to give up the last shred of dignity, wanting to move her bowels in private. Though she was always in such impeccable control of everything, she died soiled and alone on the floor. No one should have to die alone.

The last time I was with her, she was very weak. I bought her a pinwheel and horn for her walker... a little bit of wildness never hurt anyone. She was weak and confused a lot. I actually enjoyed taking care of her. The circle came round and closed as I fed her, gave her a bath, and washed the same breasts that had nourished me, diapered and swaddled her in softness as she had done for me four and a half decades before. She was embarrassed at first, but when I told her about the grace of coming full circle, she smiled softly and relaxed in my arms.

When I tucked her into bed, she began to shiver fiercely and I crawled under the covers with her, and made another circle of my arms, sharing my warmth and rocking her. I found myself crooning, "Ahhh, ahhh, baby," as my father used to do for me when I was scared. Gradually, the bone chills settled down. She rolled over and looked at me with cocker spaniel eyes and said in a papery thin voice, "I was wrong, Dawna." That was all. She closed her eyes and fell asleep. It was the last gift she ever gave me.

She never explained which, of all the right ways and right things she had taught me, she was referring to. Did she mean she was wrong about spending so much of her precious time washing the kitchen floor or writing sympathy cards or putting up with my father's abuse? Maybe she meant she was wrong never to have worn the silk and lace blouses, nightgowns, and slips that my sister and I had bought for her. Weeks after she died, when I cleaned out her dresser, the drawers were full of them, still wrapped in the original tissue paper. She knew we would find them after she was gone. They were too good for her, she told us. *Schmates*, old rags, were good enough for her. Was that what she was wrong about?

Cancer has taught me that one thing she was wrong about was death. It did not go away, even when she ignored it. And fear didn't go away either. Or pain. They just got driven deeper, and locked behind the walls around her poor, numb heart.

Driving away from the cemetery, I decided to do what she never would have dared. I had a little conversation with Death. I explained that I knew I couldn't control how or when it came, but I definitely did not want to die like my mother, with my heart imprisoned behind those walls.

It whispered, "Do you want to die numb?"

"No!" I hissed back. "I'd rather die soft and feeling pain than hard, brittle, and numb. I want to die with my heart free, wide open, wondering and loving fiercely!"

The response was immediate: "Then how do you have to live so you can be sure to die that way?"

My mother's death gave me a better place from which to live.

What she loved survived that ugly and undignified ending. It taught me that the will to live and the will to love are intertwined.

I wonder if she knows that I'm now doing what she never could or would. Here, alone in this cabin in the middle of winter, exploring the complexities of interiority, I have found a twisted seed of passion she passed on to me—the seed of denial. Whenever she hurt or was afraid, she turned herself to ice. She left her body, pretended there was no pain or fear. I can see her shrug her thin shoulders now and hear her saying, "If you can't do anything about it, why bother feeling it?"

Up here on this windy mountaintop under this immense white sky, where everything is frozen into dormancy, I am melting my commitment to stay attached to her by ignoring what hurts. Or ignoring despair. Or ignoring fear. If I feel the energy in my body, and don't tell myself any stories about it, if I follow it all the way, drifting down and down until I touch soil where the pain and fear can root, what will it become in the spring? Could that twisted seed of passion, denial, become the full, ripe seed of presence, of coming to my senses, the place where passion abides?

I am letting the ice walls around my heart soften. I am learning not to ignore or abandon myself when I am in pain. In some ways I am orphaned now that the twisted seed isn't an umbilicus. I am an orphan who is also free now to live abandoned and fully alive. Like me, were you taught that you shouldn't enjoy anything too much or be too passionate because you'll hurt too much when you lose it? Whether or not we enjoy it, we lose it. We'll lose it all. All the more reason to enjoy our passion, to love what we love, and store it up, so we'll be strong enough to stay present with the pain of loss when it comes.

Fear is passion without breath. How do we mother our passion? To be fully alive, we have no choice but to finally move closer toward what we usually veer away from. I have habitually ignored the black hole into which everything seems to disappear, the sterile void that, in my worst moments, I am afraid is at my core. It causes me to approach life as if I always had to escape from some danger.

What would it be like to open our hearts to our fear, to befriend it with wonder, as one would a deer in the forest? What if you could bring it right into the hearth of your awareness instead of ignoring it and thus allowing it to become an undifferentiated mass of demons that gang up on you in the murk? Stuffed behind walls, fear becomes a horde—the Demons of Doubt who will trample you under stories of what others think, of your endless failures, impending humiliation, and lost control. Together and ignored, they will drive you out of your own life. But when you invite them into the layered light of your awareness, they can't join together and rule you from the shadows.

I am practicing opening to fear as often as I can when it arises. I awkwardly release the constrictions and control I usually use to numb the fear out. Breathing in and out, I slowly become present to myself and my body, coming to my senses as I would with a terrified baby, noticing my breath, noticing sensations, refusing any interpretations. I imagine the warmth of compassion sinking deep into the cold place where all of that fear and confusion lives, as if a woodstove is lit on a frigid hard morning. The warmth from the stove fills the room, transforms the cold.

I imagine Wonder Woman here teaching all of us. She holds fear at the edge of the unknown, which just happens to be our growing edge, what we most need to learn. She peers over. She feels fear, but she also feels alternating currents of fascination. A bubble appears over her head as she asks, "What am I more curious about than I am afraid of?"

There is something highly passionate about living in conscious relationship to fear. I have been practicing daily by venturing into the unknown and risking a reach. Not just any old risk. Only interesting ones. Sometimes I do it on skis or snowshoes, crossing snowy terrain in early morning or right after sunset when there is a huge tense blackness in the world, when the wind seems like a language the mountains are speaking, when my wild feet break new white snow and write messages in large, exuberant prints.

Sometimes I do it with paint on blank paper, not trying to make anything, but rather just for the experience of noticing what happens on that edge of uncertainty, what emerges from the black hole of the unknown. Sometimes I just sit still with my eyes, hands, and ears empty, letting my thoughts warp, floating in the space between my breaths, my periphery getting wider and wider as it does at the ocean.

These little practices with risk and reach, fear and promise at my edge give me daily shots of vitality, the pump of adrenaline. Everything else disappears, including any notion of identity or roles or images of who I'm supposed to be. There is only the experience of being passionately alive. Still, each time, prior to setting out, fear seems more justified than trust.

The hardest thing is to keep your horizons open, to keep exploring that green growing edge. As I tremble there, I find myself wondering, "What do I love more than I fear? How can I motivate myself by what I love?"

When I die, I want to remember the pulse of life. I want to be well practiced in letting go over the edge of the known, holding on to that golden Wonder Woman rope woven of threads of love, and feel it untwining into a thousand directions.

When I die, I want my heart and soul fully seeded with rich stories and experiences. I want to be moving forward, falling upward, leaving my body well worn. I want to know presence, staying with what is hard until it softens, staying with what is narrow until it expands. I want to know how to float in the silences between breaths and thoughts. I want to know how to lift above and sink below the flow of life, to drift and dream in the currents of what cannot be known. It's not so much about being prepared for death as it is being full of life. I want to be so well practiced in crossing thresholds that dying is merely another step in the dance. I want to be so comfortable with stillness and silence that I can root in them.

And you, my friend? I am wondering, if you were writing these pages, if you crossed a chasm of hesitancy and there were an immense release in you, what words would flow from your pen, after beginning the sentence, " When I die, I want. . ."

May we all learn how to love well. May we all find something to love that is larger and more powerful than anything we fear.

How do we walk through the door of inertia to find our passion? I know that passion breaks us open until there is no partition between our body and the body of the world. I know it acts on us until something takes root inside and insists on growing. I usually forget that it begins as a reaching down into the dark of inertia as well as up and out toward the light.

CHAPTER 7

Unimagined Bridges

"We are part of the whole which we call the universe, but it is an optical delusion of our mind that we think we are separate. This separateness is like a prison for us. Our job is to widen the circle of our compassion so we feel connected with all people and situations."

—ALBERT EINSTEIN

ANDY AND I HAD JUST ARRIVED IN INDIA. We had been invited to visit the Dalai Lama. I had been rehearsing for months: I smiled kindly at anything broken—sidewalks or people who were home-less. I sat in full lotus watching the news on CNN and practiced seeing what was right about everything that seemed wrong. I meditated three times a day, mindfully noticing and releasing the desires that floated across the littered landscape of my mind. In each daydream that distracted me, the Dalai Lama recognized me as the reincarnation of a Buddhist deity. I was instantly enlight-ened and scattered seeds of love on all sentient beings. By the time our plane landed in New Delhi, I was even smiling compas-sionately (and humbly) to the cockroaches in the Ladies' Room of the airport.

Savitri, our friend and experienced guide, warned us on the landing strip not to give money to any of the people in the streets who would be begging, especially the children, but to give instead to the local charities. She explained that supporting beg-ging would encourage the continuation of an abusive system where children were often maimed so that they would "earn" more money from tourists.

For the two days we traveled by car to Dharamsala, I kept pulling back into myself each time I saw someone begging in the streets of cities or villages. There were a thousand opportunities to shut down, and I used every outstretched hand, each pleading eye to clamp down on myself. It was a very long and arduous car ride. I readily remembered selfishness and practiced it merci-lessly.

Then the rattling, rusting, black sedan we had hired finally screeched to a halt in front of a Tibetan guesthouse. As I climbed the two dark flights to our room, I noticed that all the muscles and tendons in my body were torqued and rigid. I had pulled myself in so far that I had isolated myself from the experience of a country and people I had traveled halfway around the world to visit. Not exactly the kind and compassionate person I wanted to bring to the Dalai Lama.

Upon rising the next morning, I made a promise to myself that, though I would give no money to begging children, I would give them the gift of my attention. I pulled on a sweater and, as I opened the door, I noticed a beautiful envelope had been slipped under it. It informed me that the Dalai Lama was ill and would not be able to see us, but that a Rinpoche who had been one of his teachers would meet with us later that afternoon. My heart plummeted. The cold stone floor was covered with a thousand shards of every fantasy and desire I had been carrying in my mind for months. Who cared about a ratty old Rinpoche anyway? It was the Dalai Lama or nobody.

I trudged out of our guesthouse in a shroud of gray gloom. My back felt curved with the weight of failed hope. The landscape all around me closed in, colors faded, the clouds pressed down. Each foot weighed ten pounds. I felt the desolate and disconnected emptiness of inertia.

I barely noticed a small girl approaching me, her hands outstretched, palms open. She was painfully thin, maybe six or seven years old. Her hair, eyes, and skin were all the same dusty brown as the burlap wrap she wore. Her legs and arms were like spindles, and as she came closer, the missing three fingers from her left hand and two from her right indicated she probably had leprosy. My morning's commitment rose in my mind like a red sun through dark clouds. Without another thought, I found myself scooping her up in my arms. Her eyes flashed as she threw back her head and giggled. If they could have spoken, they would have said, "Will you let me love you?"

It was one of those moments when everything I had been taught, all my beliefs and manners, attitudes and values, fell away. I had no idea what to do or what to say. All I could feel was a rising and opening in the center of my chest, as if my sternum were cracking. What emerged was as much of a surprise to me as it was a mystery to her.

I don't often sing. As a matter of fact, I don't sing if a single other living being is anywhere within earshot. It's something that has been drilled into me by my family, teachers, friends, and sundry pets. I learned that it was an act of kindness to spare them the experience of my unique tonal system. But this was a moment when all rules were broken, when no preparation or rehearsal was possible. My mouth had a mind of its own—the mind of my heart—which the giggle of this little ragamuffin had broken wide open. A song I had learned from an Alaskan woman, Libby Rodericks, spilled out:

> *How could anyone ever tell you*
> *You are anything less than beautiful*
> *How could anyone ever tell you*
> *You are less than whole?*
> *How could anyone fail to notice*
> *That your loving is a miracle*
> *How deeply you're connected to my soul.*

As I sang, my right hand signed the words the way Sandy, a woman from Wisconsin who worked with deaf children, had taught me. My eyes began to leak tears down my cheeks. I'm sure she couldn't understand the words, but in that one moment, we knew each other completely. With the two dirty fingers of her left hand, she reached over and pinched a tear from my cheek and then brought it to her lips to kiss. For a second, the world seemed to pause, to sigh. And then it was over. She giggled, and wiggled herself out of my arms, not even stopping to turn around as she ran off.

I walked slowly on, aware for a moment of my very full heart. It felt as if it had a new chamber. By the time I reached the corner of the street, however, I noticed something else. Inside my head I heard a very distinct voice from the past—my mother's—that was warning me in no uncertain terms to wash my hands and face immediately. Didn't I know that leprosy could be contagious? I smiled in amazement at the cobwebs hiding in my mind. Still, it did seem as if my fingers were tingling and becoming numb....

Passion is the capacity to touch and be touched, to reach out and to let in. This little brown child, whose name I will never know, broke my heart so wide open that it could have contained the whole world. From her, I learned that passion is a river. If you break the word apart, it becomes three words: *Pass I On*. So I am passing her on by telling the story of that moment in which we connected. For that is what passion does. It creates the desire to reach, to pass on to the world what you love. And through that opening, the world passes into you.

This precious muddy muppet is one of my inner advisors. There are hundreds of them, some I have met, some I have known, and some I have read, but I have made them all my friends, and they serve as holograms to the wisdom that has been offered to me in my life. These inner advisors who live in the honeycomb of my mind help me dissolve the barriers I build around my heart. And each reminds me that even in the moments when I feel the most helpless to "do" or fix or help, I can still, always, love in simple and ultimate ways. I can let in, let be, or be with, opening and experiencing what life brings to me.

I'd forgotten that recently. I came here to reignite my passion and mostly what I'd felt had been inertia and apathy, collapsed like bread dough without the yeast. So today I awoke in the sprawling darkness of the morning to go for a snowshoe and watch the sunrise over the shoulders of the mountains. The darkness felt right, darkness of nature, darkness of spirit, darkness of not knowing. I trudged through the woods, more at ease than I am even in the cabin. Being in them is not an escape, but a return of some kind. I stood and watched the sun float up into the world. Bronze light rose from the dark horizon.

I needed someone to talk to. Actually I needed someone to complain to, so I brought one of my inner advisors to mind. I called on my friend Rae because her cheeks always smell like Dove soap, and being with her automatically brings my breath deeper in my belly, as if my heart knows that with her, it can rest and wonder.

When I complained to her about the sludging, the total inertia, the doubts that I could ever feel passion again, a mass of wet snow slid off a spruce branch and fell at my feet. Then Rae said softly in my mind, "Of course. If you are writing about evoking passion, you first have to become aware of all the ways you are *not* passionate, the inertia that hides on the other side of passion.

Without that shadow, how can you create a true relationship with your own bright fire?"

Another inner advisor, a physicist named Neils Bohr, said that the opposite of a profound truth is not a lie, but rather another profound truth. That's why, in order to know passion, we must also know its opposite truth. Only this way can we craft lives that are wider, fiercer, and more tender, where there is space for the discovery of what can be possible.

Thinking this way, inertia becomes... what? We have to drop the label. We have to welcome the energy instead of pushing it away. We have to soften our awareness and open to it instead of building walls of ignorance around it. We have to relate to it the way I learned to from my little brown friend in Dharamsala.

My heart is willing but my mind is skeptical. Maybe yours is too. I don't ask it to give up its skepticism, just to be open and curious about what limits passion and what liberates it.

I remind myself to come to my senses. The inertia feels heavy, dark, pulling me ... down into darkness ... the way I feel when I let everything go and fall into sleep. Could inertia be passion's sleep? Passion is so vital, so awake. A sun rising. Inertia is a sinking darkness. Could it be passion's sunset?

Perhaps inertia is a twisted form of a larger intelligence. If we only experienced passion, we would be bold beyond belief, but we would burn, burn, burn ourselves out in a rapturous relationship with the part of us that is untamable. We also need the dark, the stillness, the quiet of the night for the stars and constellations, the patterns of movement of the whole universe to be visible.

How can you light a candle without casting a shadow? How can you make divisions between what is acceptable and what is not in the natural, indivisible world? Would you have sunrise but no sunset? Can there be the dynamism of passion without the receptivity of rest?

I listen to the silence I have in the past called, inertia. What I hear is almost a voice in the hollowness. It is almost a hunger, a keening in the emptiness. Not the kind of hunger of the body that my little friend from India knew. But it is very familiar to me now that I stop and listen. I have heard it for years as I sat with people who were searching for meaning in their lives. It is the sound of sacred hungers, the desire to germinate that is within every seed in the soul. It is the calling of talents and potentialities that wait to bud in the dark recesses of ourselves, beneath the static and cacophony of everyday life.

The more I listen, the more I can hear these hungers echoing in the stillness. They seem to be calling for a few basic soul needs to be filled: to express and receive love; to be present with and for what we love; to know and be known; to be peaceful and satisfied; to create peace and satisfaction; to be acknowledged as making a difference and to acknowledge that others make a difference to us; to find meaning and purpose in life as well as having life find meaning in our existence.

If you move very fast and stay very busy and live in a very noisy way, never relating to inertia or the truth stillness can bring, you may never even hear these hungers. But if you let yourself be as still as a big old spruce tree in the middle of a virgin forest, if you are willing to explore the dark shadows on the other side of passion, you will hear them too. Because the seeds of life that are in all of us want to expand outward. The shell around each seed that grows thick to protect it must crack if the seed is to sprout.

What is known and familiar must fall away. And just as you can her your stomach grumbling when your body is hungry, so, when the shell gets too thick, if you listen really deeply in the silence, you will hear your soul keening. Sacred hungers keep pushing at our edges, wanting us to let go of the old ways we have kept ourselves secure so we can expand into blossoming the life-force of what we love.

I don't know the name of that little brown child. But I haven't forgotten her. I wish I could tell her how her fingerprints are on my heart and how I cannot live in the same way I did before she pinched that tear off of my cheek. In remembering her, I remember how passion, because it is the energy of the life-force, never abandons us. Sometimes though, in forgetting to relate to our need to open and let the world into our hearts, we abandon our passion.

I am wondering about you now, dear reader. When you are very still in a place without words, steeped in silence, when the world is elsewhere with its noise and motion, what are the sacred hungers that echo inside of you?

May we all open our hearts to ourselves in wonder, and respond to the call of our passion. May we find the courage to follow its path.

How do we reignite our passion after immense loss and grief? I'm coming to understand that this isn't something we achieve or learn or even earn. The realization that the source of passion is inside leaves me knowing that it is within our sphere of influence to recover, reclaim, and rekindle it. Crisis can force us deep enough to find that source in whatever we truly love. The deeper the channel that pain carves into our souls, the greater the capacity we have to allow the river of joy to run through us.

CHAPTER 8

Rekindling the Flame

"In times of crisis, people reach for meaning.
Meaning is strength. Our survival may depend on
our seeking and finding it."
—VICTOR FRANKL

WE HAD JUST CLEARED ALL THE CHAIRS OUT OF THE ROOM, and people were placing various cushions on the gray and white speckled linoleum of the classroom. The cinderblock walls were painted that very pale green that is only found in colleges, military barracks, and mental institutions. It was going to take a miracle to teach a workshop entitled, "Finding Your Passion: Rekindling the Flame" in this sterile box.

I called on the spirit of Victor Frankl, and, as much to remind myself as any of the twenty-four other people in the room, I wrote, "It's not the events in your life that determine who you are, it's how you choose to respond to them" on the board behind me. Before I could dust the yellow chalk off my hands, before Andy could ring the bell or say good morning, there was a knock on the door. A thin woman wearing a nun's black veil leaned in, excused herself, and whispered that there was an urgent call for Dr. Markova.

I followed her thick-heeled shoes down the hall to a pay phone hanging on the wall next to the glass-enclosed office, where three other nuns were sitting at desks typing. There were names and phone numbers written in pencil on the white and blue speckled Formica wall behind the phone. I traced over them with my index finger, and hesitated long enough to take one breath before picking up the receiver that hung from the silver cord. I recognized my friend Dale's voice at once. It's always throaty, husky.

"Dawna, I have very bad news." Each word was carefully annunciated.

I didn't want to hear anything about David being hurt. "David . . . is David. . . ?"

She answered before I could finish the sentence." David's fine . . . really, he's OK. It's just that there has been a fire."

I stepped back, and glanced at the crucifix above the office door.

"My God. Don't lie to me now, Dale. Is David hurt? Has he been burned?"

"He's fine. Really. I'm sure."

I looked at the nuns in the glass office. The thin one who had come to get me smiled reassuringly. I released my breath. I would let the world go on. I could deal with anything as long as David was OK.

I don't know when Andy joined me in the hall or how I told him about the fire. Andy. This was the second home of his that had burned. The color bleached out of his face and he reached for the phone to call Gene Brownell, the farmer down the road. Good old Gene. Big, solid, Gene who could arm-wrestle men half his age and twice his size. Gene with arms that could lift two hay-bales at a time. Gene who could take care of anything. Gene would go to the house and find David. He'd wrap those arms around David and hold him until we got there.

As we rushed out of the classroom a few minutes later to leave for the airport, someone reached for my hand and placed a card in it. "Take this. I just got it in the mail from a friend in Michigan. It says, 'My house burned down. Now I can see the moon rising.'"

I held on tight to Andy's large, sturdy hand in the airplane, choosing each breath, saying over and over to myself, "It's not the events that happen to you, it's not the events that happen to you. . . ." My mind kept leaping ahead, wanting to leave the airplane behind. It was practicing by wandering through our house room by room, preparing for the loss. As I thought about each of the things that would be gone, I squeezed Andy's fingers and then released them, practicing. The big box in my closet with all the photographs of David as a baby. Squeeze. Release. At least I still had David. The blue recipe book from Temple Beth El with all of my mother's recipes in her funny, slanted, left-handed writing. Squeeze. Release. I knew most of them by heart. All the books in my office—oh my God, all of my books would be gone, my ever-faithful friends that had been my refuge for so many years, my books would be gone. Squeeze. Release. I would buy new books. My computer. I would replace it. My desk ... the manuscript. I dropped Andy's hand and protested in a very loud voice, "Oh my God, no, not the manuscript!" The man sitting on the aisle coughed, turned away, and fumbled with his *Wall Street Journal*. Andy leaned over and began to rub my back.

"You don't understand," I said. The man on the aisle flinched as if my words struck him. "That's two years of work up in smoke, literally. I never even made a copy of it. It has all of Mary Jane's handwritten edits. If that's gone, all that work is gone, all those stories of all those people I worked with are gone!"

Andy leaned over and kissed my forehead, saying nothing. I fell back against the seat, reminding myself to breathe, reminding myself that it wasn't the events in one's life that determine who you are....

My mind stopped when I wrapped my arms around David's solid body in the airport. I've read about dark falling at the end of the day, but at the end of this particular day, the dark rose—from his sweater, from his neck, from his hands—a wet and bitter darkness rising.

It must have been David who told us that there had been so many fire engines they lined the whole of West Shore Road. They were gone by the time our car pulled up, tires crunching on the gravel in front of the house. Things were too quiet for there to have been a fire. There was a thin crescent moon hanging in the sky. My father's voice whispered the poet's words in my mind, as it used to when I was little, "You were meant to carry the moon in a silver cup, the sun in a golden basket."

Maybe it was David who told us about the animals dying. Maybe it was Gene Brownell. The way the story is lodged in my mind is that before David went to work early that morning, he decided to leave our two Golden Retrievers inside. It was blustery, Bambi was old and arthritic. The cold did her no good. He decided to leave Muppet, her daughter, inside to keep her company. Domino, the calico cat, at twenty years of age, went in and out as she pleased through her own flap door upstairs. An hour later, Reverend Reeder across the street saw more smoke than usual coming from our chimney. He called the fire department, but by the time they arrived, the house was gone. Forty-five minutes and it was completely gone.

Coming home always meant a certain smell, woodsy and warm, brown and beckoning. But when we went into the house, or what was left of it, this time, there was a black plastic dead smell. This was what loss smelled like. We didn't go very far. I remember thinking it was like a movie set with walls intact on the outside but inside the caustic wetness was too thick for our flashlight beam to penetrate. Without saying a word, we turned and went back behind the house to the shed. Reffie, my horse, was standing with her head hanging down over a pile covered with a pale yellow sheet. She had no welcoming nicker for us this night. David knelt down, and as Andy shone the flashlight on the ground, he pulled back the sheet. Bambi lay on the outside, spooned around Muppet, who lay spooned around Domino, who had been David's first pet.

We all inhaled sharply and simultaneously. Suddenly it was all real. All too real. The three of us rose to our feet at the same moment that Andy murmured, "Oh my God." We grabbed each other fiercely and began to howl, to keen. In that moment, it was as if we were surrounded by every living being that had ever grieved. We huddled tight together, a closed circle of response. Under the sliver of a moon, we felt between us what none of us could stand feeling alone.

My grandmother used to tell me that daylight always brought a new beginning, but the next morning, as we entered the charcoal chasm that used to be our home, all I could find was endings. We walked silently, stopping in amazement at the phone which had melted on the only remaining kitchen wall as if it were in a painting by Salvador Dali. Each step brought a new loss. What had been the living room was now an abyss. This was where the fire had started. In the kindling bucket next to the wood stove. No one knew how or why. It didn't matter, really. I looked up. The ceiling was gone, open to the sky, except for the blackened timbers that had once supported the floor of our bedroom and my study. There was no more floor, no more bedroom, no more study or bathroom. Everything was gone—bed, rocking chair, paintings, desk, books, manuscript. How could it all be gone?

"What's that?" Andy pointed directly above our head. I followed his finger and saw the black shape balanced on the timber. He and David pulled one another up the frame of what had been the stairs until he could lean out, and, with a long arm, snatch the object. He tucked it under his jacket and they scrambled back to

me. Without saying anything they pulled me outside, across broken glass to what had been my garden, now mud and gravel.
Andy reached under his arm and pulled out my manuscript. It was
sopping wet, but as I opened it in total amazement, I could read
every word including the title, *No Enemies Within: A Creative Process
for Discovering What's Right about What's Wrong.* David leaned over,
kissed my wet cheek, and whispered, "I guess that book is supposed to be published, Mom."

A further exploration revealed that the other end of the house
had been spared as well—the garage, complete with windsurfing
equipment, and Andy's studio with keyboard and musical instruments—completely untouched. A cosmic message perhaps,
reminding us of where and how to begin again.

There's a lot more stories that vaportrail off this one. The folks
in Madison raised money for our new beginning. I insisted on
buying a small hot tub with it. We installed it in the house we
rented a few miles away. Each day after digging out the ashes and
pounding nails into boards until their hands were raw, Andy and
David came back and soaked themselves clean on the deck looking out over Lake Champlain's wide horizon. Several of our
friends came up from Boston, and we made a Solstice bonfire
under a silvery moon with some of the old charred boards from
the house and sage from that summer's garden. We cried some
more, sang songs of comfort, and told stories about phoenixes,
and things that know how to rise from the ashes.

When we finally received the insurance settlement, I decided
not to replace my lost books, but instead used the money to buy
Andy his first grand piano. It sat in the new living room that
David helped to build. The hot tub rested on the new deck, and

while we sat watching the sun set over the lake, Shaka, our new Golden Retriever, dug bones in the same place that Bambi used to. We put a big round window in my study where I wrote this story. Through it, I could see the mulberry tree we planted in the meadow over the animals' grave. And from it, I could see the moon rising over the Adirondack Mountains.

Loss strips away so much. Yet it can leave us with the understanding that the art of living passionately means learning to engage both the risk to reach as well as the grace of surrender. Mothering David, for instance, has been a process of letting go from the very first second he was born, face first, screaming and pushing his way through the no-longer-big-enough confines of my dark, watery womb into the vast expanse of air and possibility. His life-force was so strong it asked for me to let go, not my strongest suit.

I'm sure that in his last life he was a pigeon. Now that I think about it, though, maybe he was a trapeze artist, because even when he couldn't see what was coming next, he's always been willing to let go and reach. From the time he was an infant, he wanted so desperately to fly. At eight months old, he pulled himself up on the diapering table while I was on the phone in the next room, spread his chubby arms wide, and leapt off. When he hit the black tile floor, his screams were as much outrage as pain, as if he was furious that his wings hadn't worked.

It seems whenever we have followed the pattern of me letting go and his moving forward, we partner each other magnificently. When I hold on or push, when he pushes against, we struggle, Ram against Goat, horns locked, truly "butt heads." ("But David, you really shouldn't. . . ." "But Ma, I wanna. . . .")

I deeply trust that life-force that throbs so vibrantly in each of our core, that pulls us forward through every dark tunnel when it becomes too small. I have come to understand that the sorting process of grief helps us do this, if we will allow ourselves to let go of what is no more and hold on to what can be ours forever. The pain of those months after the fire made the whole winter bright, like fever, because it forced us to live so deep and hard.

I wasn't really prepared for it. Foremost among the expectations I inherited was the belief that pain was something to be avoided at all cost. The fact that each of us suffers misfortunes from time to time was my family's deepest secret. This is astounding when you consider our collective history of the Depression and the Holocaust. Nonetheless, whenever any kind of major difficulty broke through the screen of denial, each of us thought it was our fault, that in some way we were not enough, and if we were, the trouble never would have happened. Therefore we had better get busy developing ourselves into people who were enough.

We each were somewhat successful at mastering the avoidance of pain. We all failed miserably in accepting it as part of the mystery of life and learning how to grieve so that the suffering would crack us open enough for tendrils of grace to twine around the moments and events we could not control.

I read something by Doris Lessing recently that really brought this home: "Almost all humans ... have strange imaginings. The strangest of these is a belief that they can progress only by improvement. Those who understand will realize that we are much more in need of stripping off than adding on."

Loss can help us loosen our grip on all understandings of ourselves and the world so they can be rearranged into a higher and wider order. Loss can help us find and know our own strength. Loss can help us find what we truly value. Most of all, loss of any kind can help us find how much we really need each other.

Years ago, I read words from psychologist Rollo May that stay with me still. He described life as a flow, and said that without its banks there could be no river. Without loss, constraints, suffering pressing against your dreams, giving shape and direction to your destiny, you could never reach the sea. Crisis can force us deep enough to find out who we really are and what we truly love, and it is here, where there are no masks, no one else's values or beliefs, that passion lives.

Standing in the black depths of that December night, all of my stubbornness and defiance rose, flashing from my heels to my head. It was a passion as fierce as any I had known since David was born. Shivering in that frigid night I felt completely helpless to do anything, to know anything. But I felt David's heart beating, his chest heaving, and I knew that the same life-force that keeps the process of renewal alive in our bodies was already carrying us forward. I knew that if I had to die rebuilding our home, I would. And I knew that however complete the wreckage, we would find a way to make from it, the greatest possible good.

I'm sure that to successfully leap from a trapeze, you have to release your heart out into the unknown and then follow it. If you don't, you're bound to fall. That winter, I watched David learn the other side of the trapeze act, and another side of passion. I watched him learn how to catch. There was no way we could have made meaning from all of that pain, unless we caught each other in the daily fallings into the ache of all that loss. In the silence of digging in those burned-out walls, each of us had to be willing to listen to our lives, to hear them speaking to us about what really mattered. All loss has meaning, but to uncover it we have to grieve and catch ourselves in the fall into pain, giving refuge to our own aching hearts.

Among those charred remains, I discovered daily, that the more I had lost, the more I found I had. It was here I remembered the true value of love: how much risking the reach can make a difference, how much granola sent from Monty's in Madison mattered, how many times Andy's arm around my shoulders made it possible for me to bear what I had to, how often David's digging in the ashes next to Andy helped him tunnel through despair. The companionship that was there in the cold shadows brought warm streams of light.

Loss can remind us that, as human beings, we struggle with doubt and darkness in an imperfect world where suffering and grace both abound. It can teach us that our love really matters, that who we are and what we can do at our most essential level is enough.

When David was five years old, we were in St. Mark's Square in Venice. He stood covered with gray and white pigeons enrobing his arms and head. My mother whispered in the dark hallways of my mind that they were filthy creatures. But he didn't know that. He kissed each one with tender lips. As I watched, they seemed to turn into doves. Actually, pigeons are a kind of dove, but I didn't remember that until he smiled as if swathed in blessing, and kissed them.

What is loved reveals its loveliness.

Now I am wondering about the losses in your life, dear reader. What were the losses of objects, people, or dreams that took you like a kite in a strong breeze, whipped you around in a wild wind, and then dropped you right on your heels, on the ground that, ultimately, enabled you to know who you are and what you stand for?

May we all be caught by hidden hands. May the grief of our losses teach us how to live so that we love our lives as David did those pigeons.

III

Living On Purpose:
Landscapes of the Soul

"For thousands of years, sailors have used the stars to help establish their position upon the earth. We need a similar series of inner reference points to help guide us through the waves of change which are appearing on the ocean of our times. There is a name for such stars which arises out of a scientific way of depicting the world: invariant constants. Invariant constants are those qualities, processes and hidden organizing fields of life which endure throughout all changes. They are known as truth. The discovery of these invariant constants is the life task of any human being. And in the mystery of the universe, it appears that each one of us is afforded the opportunity to arrive at such constancy through our own particular journey. Stray too far from the truth and the chaos of change will tear you apart. Place your trust in it and you will find guidance though the seas may grow rough around you."

—David La Chapelle

It's 6:30 A.M. My feet crunch through the snow. I am wide awake. After four months of being in a tiny cabin that is a little world of its own, I can say more often than not that I am wide and awake. A thrush is singing with the rising sun over my left shoulder, or perhaps with the moon setting, like a circle of pale ivory over my right. I am alone and yet I feel, finally, as if I belong someplace in the world, as if I am a member of a great family, one that includes ravens and elk and aspen trees turning into pink pillars of light.

As the circle of the day turns and the vast, wide sky darkens, I go out to walk under the studded light of the stars. I am thinking about how many people live with an overwhelming sense of emptiness, not because they don't have enough in their lives, but because they lack a sense of inner guidance. It is a dark time when so many of us think too small, so many are confined by their beliefs in their own inadequacy, and so many have lost faith in themselves. It's not pain in itself that's so hard on our souls, but the meaningless suffering that comes from feeling disconnected from a sense of purpose.

I look up and see the only constellation I recognize besides the Big Dipper, Orion the Hunter. I imagine it speaking to me: *I have always been brave and noble. When I was killed, I was transformed into this constellation. You cannot see me in the ordinary way, looking at single stars one by one. You cannot see me in the light of day, though I am here all the time. You can only find me by hunting for the whole pattern in the dark, letting your eyes go wide, searching for the connections between things. I am here to encourage you to chose, chose to claim your own life. Never give anyone else responsibility for it. It is yours to make. Stay faithful to the hunt for what is original and authentic in you. Life is infinite. Use the yearnings of your heart and soul as you use me to orient like a radar beacon, a homing device. You have nothing but yourself with which to make or unmake the world.*

As I watch Orion move slowly above me, I realize that purpose is like a constellation—it can only be glimpsed in darkness, but it is always there, a homing device of the soul. Author and teacher Meg Wheatley asks her students, "Do you think your life's purpose is something you create or discover?" She suggests that rather than arguing about which is the right answer, they live as if each were true for a week and notice the effect of their experiment.

I have been doing just that. To begin with, I had to define what I thought purpose was. My mind was filled with echoes from my childhood: "Mommy, I didn't mean it." "Please, Daddy, don't hit me, I didn't do it on purpose." Since uncovering purpose is a process of "in-forming"—shaping oneself from the inside out—and the natural language of the soul is the image, I realized I'd have to turn to my intuitive mind to get a clearer sense of my reason for being. I knew I wasn't searching for a twelve-word "vision statement." Rather, I needed to hunt for a felt sense, a radar beacon. Just as geese have an internal capacity to follow coastlines and the magnetic resonance of the Earth to tell them where to go, I was looking for a guide through the journey to soul-making.

For a week, I chose to think that I created my purpose. My drawings were tight, sterile, angular, pressured, as if I were afraid I might not get "it" or get it wrong. For the next week, I assumed that, like an apple tree, I was born with a gift hidden in the seeds of my soul, hidden in what I love. I assumed the whole community needs me to bring the gift to it. I noticed an immediate freeing up of vital energy. My drawings were luminous, full of wild, vital colors, and always incomplete circles. The circle is a symbol of the Divine, of wholeness. As I looked at these drawings, I thought of each one of us as a different point on the circle, a different perspective and aspect of the life-force. And I thought of purpose as the pattern of activating intelligence that guides life, the yearning each of us carries inside to connect that circle, creating meaning and wholeness.

No one can tell you how to find your purpose. It can only be found, slowly, in your own dark sky, in whatever is sacred to you, be that church or woods. It can't be found by searching around for a role model or learning how cultural heroes handled their difficulties. It is seldom found by following anyone else's rules. It lives in the rest in the place where music is born, the fertile void, the silence between notes. It is simple and basic. It emerges slowly as a sunrise, as we search through our gifts, our darkness, our losses and loves. Your job and mine is to be quiet and alone from time to time. To be present to ourselves and the natural world, and to be in conversation with what is hidden in us in such a way that we can explore what brings us more alive.

I reread my journals for the past few months, searching for patterns, the constellation of coherence that purpose. I began to see it in the last section of each journal entry, where I end with an aspiration. On November 15, I wrote, "May I grow in wisdom and learn how to love better." On December 8, " May I widen my circle of compassion." On January 17, "May I recognize the essence of who I am and help it to manifest in the world." Then three times in February, there are variations on a theme: "May I help heal the wound between the intuitive and analytic ways of thinking." Repeatedly, as in a symphony, I found the recurring theme of wanting my work to be a mirror for the beauty I find in people, showing them the secret and lovely things that they are afraid to believe about themselves.

Then I read something by Rachel Naomi Remen that sent a vibration through my mind, cracking it wide open. When things settled, nothing was in quite the same place as it had been before. She said, "We are not broken, we are just unfinished." Suddenly I realized that my future was not a series of damaged places that I needed to fix. Rather, my life was a work of art waiting to be completed. As the dust settled, I knew the structure for my inquiry. I pulled out my big journal and wrote down four very evocative questions that I had known for some time, but which I had never before realized were guides to uncovering a sense of purpose: What's unfinished for me to give? What's unfinished for me to heal? What's unfinished for me to learn? What's unfinished for me to experience? It is through exploring these questions that the constellation called purpose began to be revealed.

What's unfinished for you to give? In the thousands of moments that string together to make up our lives, there are some where time seems to change its shape and a certain light falls across our ordinary path. We stop searching for purpose, we become it. Looking back, we might describe these moments as times when we were at our best, when the gifts we were born with and the talents we have developed were braided with what we love and the needs of the world.

CHAPTER 9

The Spot of Grace

"If you bring forth what is within you, what you bring forth will save you. If you do not bring forth what is within you, what you do not bring forth will destroy you."

—JESUS, GOSPEL OF SAINT THOMAS

SOME WORDS JUST DON'T LEAVE ME ALONE. They attach themselves to my heels like Peter Pan's shadow and follow me through the strip malls of my mind. They follow me until I'm willing to get curious about their message and meaning. For a very long time, so long I'm embarrassed to tell you, the word attached to my right foot was *educare.* I ignored it the way I do dreams sometimes, figuring it was just my mind playing with the noun that described what I did for years in classrooms. Little did I know I was supposed to get curious about the root of the verb, which means "leading out that which is within," and it would become a branch of my life's purpose.

The word stuck on my left foot was *grace.* I ignored that one even longer, because where I grew up, Jewish people don't even think about grace. To understand what grace finally led me to, I have to tell you about my grandmother, and what she taught me about walking, which was really more about finding your purpose than it was about physical fitness. She explained that we all walk a spiral path she called the wisdom trail, and we walk on the foot of risk, then the foot of mastery, then back on the foot of risk. As I understood it, if a person stays on the foot of risk too long, they find themselves nervously hopping from thing to thing, never settling in and developing mastery. On the other hand, if they stay in their mastery too long, they get stuck in the mud and their soul never really gets to develop fully.

Each time we shift from the foot of mastery to the foot of risk it takes a leap of faith, a little gasp in the unknown where God can enter.

Maybe that's where grace comes in.

Since my parents were rather nebulous about religion, I wasn't made into a devout anything. This gave my imagination lots of freedom to create meanings for things that had to do with the divine. But when a question such as, "What's a soul?" would itch in my mind as bad as the chicken pox, and my reasonable parents couldn't answer to my satisfaction, I'd ask my grandmother, who spoke words that were beyond reason. Sometimes it was because her language was a patois of Russian, Yiddish, and Hell's Kitchen-Immigrant, but usually it was because she had a different attitude than most reasonable people. She was nothing like the teachers in my school, who were mostly like dusty libraries, stuffed full of knowledge. Her mind was much more like a spacious palace of discovery.

One Friday morning, when I was seven, the question about what a soul was had created rashes in my mind. We were in her tiny kitchen, sitting at the red oil-cloth covered table. She was making challah, golden Sabbath egg bread, and as she braided the dough, I blurted out the soul question. She stared out the window beyond the lines of wet laundry as if searching mysterious landscapes I couldn't see. Finally, she said, "Some people think we're born with sin in our souls. I don't think that." She patted the rising dough, and then raised her thin white eyebrows, looking directly at me. I waited expectantly for a further explanation, but instead, she shook her head ever so slightly, and pointed a thin floury finger at me. "Live for a few days as if your body were inside of something called *neshuma*, a soul, that wants to rise and reach...." Her eyes twinkled, and while sprinkling poppy seeds lavishly over the surface of the bread, she continued, "Then, for a few more days, live as if there were no such thing as *neshuma*, no mystery in the world or in you. When you come back next week, tell me what you discover."

The first few days were easy. It was like spring: the air was charged with sweetness, the days full of birdsong and yellow shimmering, everything seemed like a riddle. The next days though felt thin and bare, flat as dough that wouldn't rise. My mind braided what her deft hands taught me into the definition. To this day, I think of a soul as being heavily seeded, and grace as the yeasting that happens when there's a crack, a gasp, where *neshuma* can rise and enter the mysterious landscape we call the world.

As I look over my life, it seems that my footsteps of risk and mastery always seem to be about *educare,* and finding the spot of grace inside the soul of people. I haven't been able to say this is what I was doing until recently. It is just what would happen when I met someone and opened myself up to them. My mind started doing its discovery thing: Where is that spot of grace? How can I knead it so it will rise? How can I help bring forth what's hidden inside them?

When I was in school, education seemed to have nothing to do with *educare* or grace, or even soul for that matter. My twenty-five-year education focused on filling empty vessels with stuff, as in sticking flowers into a vacant vase. I was taught to give instructions, to reason, to track mistakes as if they were failures. The more education I "got," the more I was trained in the history of pathology—how people get sick and crazy. But all that helped me do was make people sick and crazy.

This was contrary to what I had learned with my grandmother. If you watch a baby learn to grab a cup, there is a natural path they follow. They reach out and search. First, they get oatmeal. They reach out again, and get Mommy's hair. They reach out one more time and get cup. After one more handful of oatmeal, it's cup, cup, cup. The natural human learning process is to track success and discard mistakes.

I've always gravitated toward people who, in one way or the other, were stuck. In my mind, this means they were disconnected from their own resources or radar beacon: kids in the inner city or migrant labor camps, kids who were judged and labeled by all the oatmeal and hair they had gotten their hands into. But that path only led me to frustration. I began keeping track of my own failures, and I wanted to give up like everyone else.

That ended in a migrant labor camp in Florida. I was hired as a learning specialist, which meant keeping the kids no one else could teach out of trouble. My office was a small, dark room that was also the janitor's supply closet. A boy named Jerome broke me open. He was fifteen, in fifth grade, twice as big as I was, and labeled as being too retarded to learn and too disruptive to be with other kids. The first thing he said to me was, "You ain't gonna make me read." Hey, I wasn't stupid. This kid had fists bigger than my purse. It was clear I wasn't going to make him do anything. I did what I learned from my grandmother. I searched for the spot of grace in his soul.

It's really nothing more complicated than the act of noticing and cherishing. In Jerome's case, I noticed that he was anything but empty or stupid. He was the chess champion of the migrant labor camp. He played brilliantly, literally. No matter who his opponent was, he shone. The chessboard was his natural field of mastery, and it became obvious that all I needed to do was find a bridge between what he knew about playing chess and learning to read.

What motivated Jerome to play was the love and challenge of the game. So I left a thick book with lots of photographs and gold letters on its cover: *A History of Black America*, on my desk, and bet him that if we played a game of chess and I won, he would learn to read it. If he won, I would read it to him. Knowing I was seriously remedial in the game, he took the bet, with what could only be divine intervention, I won. (The only time I have ever won a game of chess!) I taught him to read the way he played chess—through his body, then his eyes, and in silence. In a few short months he went from a "retarded illiterate" to a shining and obsessive reader. He taught me that there are many ways people have of processing information, many learning patterns, instead of the one I had been taught in education classes. From this root sprouted my life's work in intellectual diversity, which I've researched, taught, and written about for thirty-five years.

Jerome never became an A student. Chances are that he dropped out of school. Chances are that he's either in a prison or dead by now, but whether in a cell or heaven, I'd be willing to bet that he's still reading, and that he knows he's not dumb.

When any of us are stuck up against our limitations, like Jerome, we are disconnected from our spot of grace. No small wonder— from the time we begin school, if not sooner, we are taught to be blind to our assets and only see our deficits. We are carefully marked on how many we got wrong on a test and, rarely if ever, asked how we know how to spell the ones we got right. By the time we are adults, we are well versed in every one of our limitations, skilled in our incompetence. If we were fish in an aquarium, it would be as if we kept smashing against the glass, and forgot the fact that we were perfectly capable of turning ever so slightly and swimming gracefully in the water all around us.

Aristotle said that one's purpose is merely a matter of knowing where one's talents and the needs of the world intersect. The ancients recognized that cultivating, developing, and setting free one's gifts was the essential labor of one's life.

The things I was taught to be most ashamed of—my illiterate father, my stubbornness and refusal to accept what authority figures told me on face value, my fascination with how the glass could be half-full, my wild imagination, my curiosity with synthesizing diverse elements into a new system, my ardent loyalty to anything injured or maligned—are all essential resources in finding and nurturing my purpose.

Finding that spot of grace in people, searching for what could be right about what everyone else said was wrong, always left my soul singing. It was my radar beacon.

Remember when we were kids and played "Hotter, hotter, colder, colder"? I'm not sure what you called it where you lived, but it's basically the same children's game all over the world. Without knowing it, when we played that game, we were deeply involved in the spiritual practice of finding and following our purpose: If it's hot, do more of it. If not, discard it.

When I ask corporate leaders, classroom teachers, or gas station attendants to describe themselves at their best, they hem, haw, stutter, and give me a brief qualified statement such as, "Well, I'm not too bad at inspiring some people to do their best, given that times are good and I have adequate back-up, and of course if I have a leadership team I can work with, and I've been working at being more assertive, but it's very difficult because. . . ." If I had, on the other hand, asked them to tell me of their areas that needed improvement, chances are they would have been very articulate and answered without hesitation. Why not? They rehearse their deficits every night before they go to sleep. "I didn't conduct that meeting very well today, and my financials are a mess. I've got to get more organized...."

Milton Erickson used to tell his students that the best way to work with people having a problem is to find their historical pattern of success and help connect it to where they're having difficulty. Most of us, instead, connect to our limitations. When we're stuck, you can bet we have been pointing out to ourselves what's wrong and trying to think of ways to fix it instead of building on what *is* working. The simplest indicator of the ineffectiveness of this is noticing your energy level. Focus on what hasn't worked for you today and your energy will flatten or sink. Focus on the best of what you did today, and your vitality level will go up. I don't know about you, but if I were empress of the world and wanted people to find and live according to their purpose, I'd give them good feelings, and when they were off course, I'd give them a sense of emptiness and numbness.

Educare—how do we bring out of our souls those gifts we were given? The spot of grace—how do we plant these gifts in the soil of that which we care deeply about, that which matters so much to us it gives meaning to our moments?

My friend, what story of personal fulfillment would you tell me, if we were together now, the snow glittering around us like bits of fallen sky? When have you felt at your best while achieving something you were proud of? What does fulfillment feel like in your body, and what does the story you tell reveal about what's really important to you?

May we all become ambassadors for whatever we love in the human community.

What's unfinished for you to heal? Some of the obvious places to look for purpose are in the pattern of our gifts, values, and successes, but what gives texture and form to any pattern are what we often label as our failures and wounds. Our pain is often the aperture through which we can learn to trust ourselves, as well as contribute to the world in which we live.

CHAPTER 10

Let Our Wounds Be Our Teachers

"For while the tale of how we suffer, and how we are delighted and how we may triumph is never new, it always must be heard. There isn't any other tale to tell. It's the only light we've got in all this darkness."
—JAMES BALDWIN

IN YIDDISH, THERE ARE A THOUSAND WAYS TO CALL someone a fool, but only one to describe a person who is the opposite: *mensch*. A mensch is a person who lives from his or her heart, who communicates really important things to the rest of us without ever sounding Important. By the end of the Saturday afternoon session of the training program that Andy and I facilitated in Little Compton, Rhode Island, every person recognized Peris as a mensch.

It was 1993. We called the program a community of commitment because each person in the group made a commitment to serve the larger community over the year in some way they could not do without the support of the circle.

The room where we met faced west, overlooking the Atlantic. When her turn came, Peris lengthened her spine, ran her fingers once across her lips, and explained in a quiet, resonant voice, that her parents were Croatian, many of her relatives were Serbian, and the fighting was ripping her heart apart. She said that she felt called to reach out somehow to as many people as she could in the former Yugoslavia, and needed the group's support to be as clear a vehicle as possible. Her eyes glistened as if she were feeling compassion for every soft thing that walks through the world. Then she pulled up her shirt collar, the corners of her mouth twitched upward, and she said, "This reminds me of a true story...." She proceeded to tell an outrageously filthy joke in English, Serbian, and Croatian.

That evening, I was sitting by the pay phone in the hall, waiting for a call from home. There was a copy of *Time* magazine on the small mahogany table next to me. On the cover were the faces of many women with haunted eyes and scarves tightly pulled around their heads. The words underneath were "Rape in Camps in Former Yugoslavia." I quickly flipped it over so all I could see was an advertisement for Camel cigarettes. The phone rang and I spoke to David for ten minutes about the dog, the house, the homework. Then I sent him kisses, stood up, and, without thinking, slipped the magazine into the drawer of the table and closed it firmly.

Later that night, my body fell asleep immediately, but my mind kept slipping back downstairs to that mahogany table. Finally, I dragged myself down there, and brought the magazine up to my bed. I wrapped a quilt around my shoulders, breathed deeply at least six times, and looked at the picture on the cover that I had earlier so adroitly ignored. I looked at it, into it, through it. I felt as if I were a stone sunk into mud. I asked myself gently, "Why didn't I want to look? What didn't I want to see?"

Immediately my mind tumbled backward in time, and my heart, my whole body clenched. I was fifteen, lying in my own blood, being raped. I shook my head fiercely and said out loud, "No more. It's over now. I've made it. I'm safe now." And it was over. It had been over for three decades. I had worked through that rape in every form of therapy known to womankind. I had spoken of it, written of it, healed it on a cellular level. But there are some violent acts that pierce the atmosphere of one's life, leaving a hole through which the damp wind seems to blow forever. Why was it coming up again? What was its drafty message for me this time?

I shivered, let the question float above me, while I got wider, a tiny bit more curious. Then, in one instant, I knew what it was. As I looked at those women's faces, I knew that in some way I carried a responsibility. I had never told anyone the name of the man who raped me, in fear, of course, that I would be punished. Fear of retribution. All the same, I knew, in that one very clear moment, that he must have gone on to rape other women. And I knew I had some responsibility for those rapes.

"I am responsible." I whispered, "For not speaking. For not breaking the silence." Then I centered by noticing my breath. I turned all of my attention to the place in my breathing where the out-breath became the in-breath. I sank into the great wisdom of my body that knew how to let go of what is old, and take in what is fresh and life-sustaining. I placed my hand on my chest and felt compassion for myself. I had made it. I had come through that terrible time. I was not broken. But I was not finished with it either.

I felt the callus around my heart soften for the girl I had been, and for the woman I was; for the women in the refugee camps, and the women who were raped by the same man who violated me. All I could do was weep. My soul was washing itself clean. From outside my window, I heard the fierce collapse of wave after wave of the ocean. Such force, such softness and ease. I lay back and floated in the ocean of my breath. And that was enough—almost.

When I sat down in the group early the next morning, I brought the magazine cover with me. I announced my commitment to do whatever I could to help in the healing of those women. I turned to Peris, and waited until the quivering in my body eased enough to allow words to come. "Will you help me help them, somehow?" Peris nodded and came to sit next to me. She reached for my hands and whispered two words: *sestre nashe*. As she spoke, for just an instant, the whole seascape glowed red. We were held in it, all of us, held in the authentic passion and purpose of the two of us in this moment. Later, Peris wrote a haunting chant called *Sestre Nashe*, the words of which were the same in all dialects: "Our sisters, our sisters, we know of your suffering, we carry you in our hearts."

With the help of many people, Peris formed an organization called World Reach. The logo she chose was a hand reaching out with a spiral in the palm. We thought of the spiral as our community. None of us could have done what we did by ourselves. All of us, with the support of the circle, found a way for the wounds of our individual histories to be a collective doorway to living our purpose.

One of my favorite ways to find someone's spot of grace is to ask them about their favorite scar. When I first began doing it, I didn't understand why it worked, but almost every time, the person would light up as he or she unfolded a tale of gory wounding while tenderly stroking the scar. When I finally told about the time Stuie Stillman rode me on the handlebars of his two-wheeler when I was five, and one of the spokes broke and it tore a big hole in my leg that I couldn't feel until my mother pointed at it and screamed because blood was running in a stream out of my body, I understood. Scars are made of the strongest tissue in our bodies even though they are the result of deep injury.

When I ask about a scar, I ask what message or lesson came through the scar. Often times what I hear are stories of turning points—an event where we chose to turn toward or turn away from life in some way.

My parents sent my sister and me to summer camp for years. Too many years. My sister loved it. I hated it. All except Sunday mornings when we'd get to dress up in costumes and act out stories from the Old Testament. The first time I got to play Joseph and wear the fabulous coat of many colors, I felt as if I'd come home. My favorite part was when his jealous brothers, who had sold him into slavery for twenty pieces of silver, came on their hands and knees to the pharaoh's court and begged his forgiveness. I always took particular delight imagining, of course, that it was my much older sister, who had threatened to put me out for adoption, groveling, but be that as it may, my favorite part was when I got to place my hands on her head and declare in a booming voice, "Do not be afraid!... Even though you intended to do me harm, God intended it for good."

What if the moments of the greatest wounding in your life were also places where the Divine crossed your path and the unquenchable dream of your life was born? There is nothing that drives the human mind more than what is called an incomplete gestalt—an unmet need for closure of some kind. Imagine seeing a pad of paper lying near you with nothing drawn on the page but a circle that is not closed. Imagine hearing just this much of the song, "Jingle bells, jingle bells, jingle all...." Imagine an itch in a very sensitive place that you cannot reach. Purpose, ultimately, is the drive to close that circle, finish that song, scratch that itch, bridge that gap.

If your purpose is only about you, it has no branches. If it is only about the rest of the world, it has no roots. I believe this is why learning that the moments when our essential needs were not met in some very basic ways hold the possibility to unfold our gifts. I believe God has an exquisite sense of humor. Wouldn't it be a good joke if the worst that has happened to us holds the possibility of bringing the best in us to the community?

Andy taught me to ask the people I work with, "What do you love that is bigger than this wound?" One woman, a concert cellist, had been in a car accident caused by a drunk teenager that resulted in her arm being so badly damaged she could never play again. After much silence, she said, "I love being alive, learning more, and teaching others." Her grieving eventually opened up to her going back to school, getting a degree in counseling, and then working with young people arrested for DWI. Another musician, an Irish man whose childhood was pockmarked by various kinds of cruelty, created Random Acts of Kindness™ Gangs in the inner city where he lived. This is called redemption.

A wounding does not have to be the path to purpose forever. It can help us turn garbage into compost for compassion. It can serve as a canoe to help us cross great divides in our lives, places where we disconnected from trusting ourselves in the world. Ultimately, though, when we get to the other shore, it may best serve us to set the canoe down if we are to continue the journey on foot, rather than carry it on our back as a heavy burden.

And now, dear reader, I am wondering what this telling evokes for you. What wound in your life could be a passageway to your purpose? How could its healing provide a connection to the healing of the world?

May all of our wounds and broken dreams be salved. May our souls crawl from hiding places of shame and gaze upon the mystery of healing that can not be explained. May we learn to breathe our spirits alive.

What's unfinished for you to learn? We become accustomed to identifying ourselves as nouns, as small, enclosed, exclusive, and local units: artist, friend, mother. It is as if we spend so much time close to the canvas, carefully painting tiny purple dots in a Pointillist painting, that we have forgotten how to step back enough to get a sense of the whole. Yet it is only from this perspective that we can learn to see the overall patterns we have been creating, the verbs we have been living—creating, befriending, mothering,—which are the horizons we need to move toward.

CHAPTER 11

Way Closes, Way Opens

(from *Let Your Life Speak* by Parker Palmer)

"My strength is gone. When I lie down worn out, others will stand, young and fresh. By the stairs I have built, they will mount. They will never know the name of the person who made them. At the clumsy work they will laugh; when the stones roll, they will curse me. But they will mount, and on my work; they will climb, and by my stair."

—OLIVE SHREINER

MOST OF THE STORIES IN MY MIND UNFURL LIKE A RIBBON, one event spilling seamlessly into another, but not this one. My mind skips through this twenty-year-old memory as if it were one of the flat stones David used to skitter over the mirrored surface of Lake Mascoma on a fine fall day.

How in the world I could have allowed my only child, to whom I had completely devoted thirteen years of hypervigilant attention, to go to boarding school in Germany for six months? When I try to sort out what actually happened from that which *could* have happened, I fall back through a maze of images.

I am sitting behind the steering wheel of a rented black Renault in the circular driveway of a huge, old, yellow castle. I am sitting watching the windshield wipers go back and forth, relentlessly trying to keep the glass clear of falling fat drops of rain. I am sitting there, stunned, caught in the time between lightning and thunder. Finally the sky tightens around me and I drive through the black wrought-iron gates, past the cement gargoyles.

I glance in the rearview mirror. Schloss Eringergelt grows smaller by the second. Behind me, David. Ahead of me . . . what? The Autobahn. Frankfurt. Europe. Freedom. Behind me, David, in that weird yellow castle with the moat and 1,000 kids who don't speak English. My precious baby.

He's not your baby. He's an about-to-be adolescent boy who wants to go to this school. He made this decision on his own. He has a life of his own, a mind of his own.

Ridiculous! He doesn't have a mind of his own, he's just a little vulnerable being who grew inside my body, whom I am supposed to protect and take care of. I know his every thought and need.

If you knew his every thought, how come you didn't know he was plotting to go to school in Germany? He is his own person, he comes through you not for you, remember? Besides Frau Klausner had such kind blue eyes, like a Colorado sky, really, and she assured you David would be cared for as if he were her son. And he's here with his two best friends. And Herr Markert speaks English and promised you he would watch over the boys. A thousand kids go to school here and they all have rosy cheeks and are so energetic. David will be fine. Besides, he loves Wienerschnitzl. It's his favorite food.

That's what *you* say, I think to myself. Herr Markert, the *only* teacher in the school who speaks English, is the very same man who told you he left Madison, Wisconsin, five years ago because the whole country was turning Communist. This sunken-chested, soft-bellied man whose hair and politics are parted way too far to the right, who looks sixty when he's only thirty, this reactionary is the man with whom I, Emma Goldman's great-niece, leave my only child? As for all those robust children … not one of them spoke enough English to understand David if he were to say, "Stop! You're hurting me!" How many of their grandparents do you think were Nazi guards in the camps that killed my ancestors? Did you notice how they were all bigger than David? Even the ten-year-olds. Why did I let you talk me out of escaping with him last night when I had the chance?

The windshield wipers lead my mind back and forth.

Free at last. Free to follow myself, free to find my own rhythm, my own routine, my own calendar.

David, my only child, my son, what am I doing leaving him in this strange place with a moat? Did I tell Frau Klausner that he's allergic to eggs?

Free to do what I want when I want, free to define my own boundaries, to pursue my career, to have quiet in the house, to travel, to be a woman, not just a mother.

In the rearview mirror, the yellow castle is as small as a toy. The windshield wipers flop from right to left. I mumble my favorite words of Victor Frankl to comfort myself: "It is not the events in our lives that determine who we become, but the meaning we choose to place on those events." Victor Frankl reminds me that the choice is mine. Which story will I tell myself? One that leads me into a old familiar rut, or one that carries me to a new possibility?

The tears trace crooked paths down my cheeks.

After thirteen years, I am finally free to pursue my purpose. It's time to discover what my own life's orbit is like without David's gravitational field. For thirteen years, he has been the center of my existence, my very reason for holding on and staying sane. Every decision has been made on the basis of what would or would not be good for David. My life calendar is David-based: "1970? Oh that was the year when David was four, so we must have been just getting ready to go on the trip around the world."

I need to know whether or not I will disappear into a black hole in space for six months. I need to find my own edges, hear my own voice in my mind. There is nothing to hold me down anymore. I can go where I want, eat what I want, do what I want, just like all my friends who don't have children.

I find myself smiling in anticipation. In the rearview mirror, the woman I see is white-faced with blue cups of grief under her eyes. Reflected in the windshield, the woman I see has warm sugar in her veins.

After a month of attending professional conferences, sipping fine white wine, traipsing through the French Alps to the sound of cowbells; after all-night conversations about Jung and R. D. Laing and Gregory Bateson in Snowmass, and Boston, and New York, I returned home with a kidney infection and a wild urge to reorganize everything. I pulled the house apart and put it back together. I simplified. I neatened. I washed the kitchen floor and it stayed shiny for hours, days. The white silence bounced off the walls. I turned over all the mattresses in the house as well as the question of what I really wanted to do with my life.

Without David, the master of wheedling, convincing, conniving, negotiating, and manipulating, I could actually say no to people without waffling, explaining, or backing down. I began to write again. "A manual," I thought, "I'll write a creative manual to finding yourself and getting out of your own way."

I could not help notice that I felt a little hollow. In fact, when I wasn't frenzied with activity, what I really felt was inert. Everything seemed to be covered in Vaseline, blurred, like an old black-and-white movie. But at least I no longer felt pulled in so many directions. I couldn't feel a pull in any direction except down.

I had time to talk to friends on the phone—the phone was actually available to use whenever I wanted. Hours would go by when it wouldn't ring. I told all my friends and clients that no one was to call me on Sunday nights. Sunday nights were when the world slipped back into focus, when the windshield wipers cleared the view. Sunday nights were when David called.

I couldn't just sit still and listen as he spoke. I bounced off the clean, overstuffed black couch, paced back and forth on the newly vacuumed burgundy carpeting, tangled my fingers in the plastic spirals of the phone cord. I tried to draw him out with questions, but I couldn't think of any evocative enough to pull him through the cord back to me.

After a month of Sunday phone calls about soccer and the absence of Wiernerschnitzel, David called and told me that his friend Mike had decided to return home, because he was home-sick and couldn't hack it. I waited for the magic words that my son would return with him. David went on talking about soccer and how he was getting A's in English and math, but wasn't get-ting grades in the other classes because he hadn't even figured out what they were yet. I waited until my fingers were so tightly entangled in the phone cord that they began to turn as blue as my heart, and I asked, "And what about you, David? Wouldn't you like to come home now too?"

His response was hesitant, but his voice was as firm as a thir-teen-year-old boy's can be. "No, Mom. Frau Klausner says we have to keep stiff upper lips and not be crybabies. I can make it. I'll be just fine."

Did Frau Klausner have an electric tweezer attached to my son's fingernails as he was speaking to me?

"David, really. Only dead things get stiff. It wouldn't mean you're a baby or anything. You've done this for a month. You can come home." The phone cord was now twisted into an intricate macrame. I dropped my voice into as much of a whisper as I could manage across the entire Atlantic Ocean.

"David if you want to come home but can't say it because Frau Klausner is there, just cough into the phone."

No cough. Just, "Gotta go Mom. Some big kid is waiting to use the phone. Love ya."

I didn't say anything. I just began to breathe the way I had learned in Lamaze classes before he was born.

What big kid? Maybe the big kid had his hand on David's throat and he couldn't cough.

My friend Judy says that the Quakers have an expression which refers to finding one's path in life: "way opens." On that Sunday night, in some very definite way, I realized that a way was closing. I felt lost, vacant, diffuse. Find any word in a dictionary that is the opposite of *purposeful* and it would have described me that evening.

Sometime during the night I had a remarkable dream. There were no images, there was no scenario. Just words, which I then scribbled on the pad next to my bed: *What is your profession? Unlimited access. Grabbing back and bringing through the woods.* The next morning, I felt just as inert as the night before, but porous-inert instead of dense-inert. I kept thinking about the words from my dream while I showered. They echoed with my footsteps as I went for a walk around the lake. It was a surprising walk, because I noticed the gulls circling over my head, the pebbles crunching beneath my feet. The intoxicating smell of the cedar trees. I stopped and cherished it all. I hadn't noticed or cherished anything since David left. I still felt inert, but it was an open inertia now, instead of an empty one.

When I returned to my studio, I picked up my pen and began to doodle the words from my dream all over the page. *Profession. Profess in.* I stood up and went over the huge Oxford dictionary that sits open on my desk. *Profess:* "to acknowledge or declare one's faith publicly." I began to write furiously. "What do I profess faith in? This question has nothing to do with jobs. No matter what my job is, what will I acknowledge or declare my faith in?"

Immediately, my energy began to sizzle, and my hand moved with a mind of its own. "Unlimited access. I have faith that every child, every human, has a gift, specific seeds in their soul they are meant to bring to the community, and they deserve to have unlimited access to that gift. I have faith that each of us brings a unique value to the larger whole. This is my profession. If I take this on, if I give it voice and energy, every one of the days of my life will count for something. If not, every day will be wasted."

I paused long enough to take a sip of tea. My pen pulled me to the page. "*Grabbing back. Bringing through the woods.* Grabbing back what was given to us and bringing it through the 'woulds.' I would . . . if I could. I would concentrate on what's really important to me, if I could. I would write stories that would move people beyond the limitations of their previous history, if I could. I would do whatever was possible to shift people's focus to growing their strengths instead of trying to fix their weaknesses, if I could."

By now the energy running through me was so intense I was writing and pacing at the same time. "How can I bring myself through those 'woulds'? What do I need to grab back? What do I need to give myself unlimited access to?" As soon as the question mark was on the paper, the pen was scrawling a response, big, bold, one word to a page:

"My—belief—that—I—matter.

My—capacity—to—generate—my—own—joy.

My—capacity—to—ask—myself, 'What's really important to me? What do I need to give voice to?'"

Then I grabbed a thick red marker and wrote:

"Remember to ask myself what resources do I have to live on purpose, with joy!!!!!!"

I read somewhere that a writer should only use six exclamation points in their whole life. I used them all up that morning, but I began making choices as if I had unlimited access to the world's supply of exclamation points. Each morning, I re-read those pages, feeling the words, wondering how I could embody them. I wrote lists of my gifts, talents, and resources. Before I slipped into sleep, I asked myself how I could access and strengthen my gifts, instead of reminding myself how many things I should fix and correct.

Victor Frankl says that meaning precedes being. I began to live as if that were true. As if, from professing the things that really mattered to me, a new being would emerge who had her own center of gravity, and whose life had a centripetal force pulling in to that center instead of a centrifugal force dispersing out from it. In the darkness of all the apathy I had felt, the stars of a unique constellation began to appear—who I was supposed to be, no matter what. Through the loss of identity as "mother", I touched again my deeper purpose in being alive.

When David returned at last, I hugged his bony shoulders, kissed his eyelashes, and felt his heart beat against mine. But something essential had changed. The clinging response he used to give me, the melt, was gone. And the vine inside me had loosened its grip as well. He leapt over to the refrigerator, poured himself a mug of milk, an immense bowl of Captain Crunch, and spoke in German to Bambi, his precious Golden Retriever. I asked him how it felt to be home, expecting he would be as articulate with me as he had been with his dog.

He looked over to me, shrugged, popped his knuckles, and said, "Gnmph."

As if it were a precious bird, I took his hand in mine, and grew silent as the earth. I leaned my back into the front door, stared at his straight dark hair that had a special way of retaining flecks of light, and then looked over at the white wall, where my shadow was dancing in celebration.

When a "way closes" and one stage of our lives is complete, we are at an intersection, a threshold. Because we are all such creative beings in essence (yes, even those of you who swear you have no right brain), we approach the unknown, stories first. Like Rumpelstiltskin, we take any bit of straw, any fact of reality, for example, "My son is going away to school," and then either spin it into gold or dung by the stories we choose to attach to it: "He won't need me. Nobody needs me. I'm gonna go eat worms." Or "Both of us will learn whole new ways of relating to each other and the world." I call the former "rut stories" because they numb us and confirm that we always are who we always have been; and I call the latter "river stories" because I think of them as energizing, carrying us toward the possibility of purpose.

Usually we don't even realize we are telling these stories, but they shape our entire way of perceiving, believing, and relating. We all do it all the time. Just track your mind for a few minutes and see for yourself. *I'm sitting on a brown chair, watching my fingers move over the keys, hearing my nails click, tasting tea on my lips. I have to remember to get some more Earl Gray, but I really should stop drinking caffeine because it makes me crazy. Andy told me it isn't good for me, but who is he to tell me what I can and cannot do anyway....* ooops, I'm going into story. Stories gather our experience into shapes, in much the same way that a fish tank gives form to the watery reality of a carp.

Author, authentic, authenticity, authoritative all have the same root, which means genuine. When we become aware that we are telling ourselves stories, we begin to have a choice about what stories we are telling, and that is the true beginning of authoring our own existence. Rut or river, these strategies of our imagination tell us who we are, what our purpose is, and how we connect, or don't, to the whole.

As with any other great force of nature, there is both glory and danger in the stories we tell ourselves. Some are toxic and keep our problems festering. Others are tonic and bring us beyond the limitations of our previous history. To be in a life of our own definition, we must be able to discover which stories we are following and determine which ones help us grow the most interesting possibilities.

When way closes, as it did for me when my center of gravity had to shift away from David, our old stories and identities are threatened. It can feel like dying. What was falls apart, as if a shedding were taking place, but what will be has not yet emerged. This is the time, when we must relate to purpose's shadowy partner—apathy.

In my better moments, I think of apathy as purpose's sleep. In my worse moments, when I'm trying to fix it or get rid of it, I call it feeling lazy, depressed, or useless.

Ultimately, it always seems to request the same thing of us—that we withdraw into solitude as much as possible, that we integrate what was and get receptive to the authenticity of what is—our present experience, our rhythm, body, the natural world—and then to what could be needed of us by the larger community.

This sounds so simple as I just rattle it off, and it is simple, but oh, it is not easy. For if we have been caught up in a really compelling story, the loss of an old identity will bring us into the trough of the wave, where all we can hear are rumblings of our sacred hungers—the need to be loved, to have someone be present with us, to be acknowledged as making a difference, to know, to feel peace and satisfaction.

The journey from rut to river increases the porosity of the membranes that divide us from each other. If we allow ourselves permeable boundaries, we may discover that we are not as alone as we think. We may find way opening. When we touch our sense of purpose, we may discover that we are each other's destiny.

As you carry yourself forward, dear reader, I am wondering what rut stories you tell yourself. What would the river story be that would shift the pivot of your existence so that you could become more real and alive, serving your fine purpose?

May we let go of the too-small circles we have drawn around ourselves and each other. May we each create stories that will help us all actively engage with our present and future.

What is unfinished for you to experience? I had to die to know how much I really wanted to live. Not as in living longer, but as in living deeper, wider. As a result of this one experience, those few moments of clock time, being alive transformed from a train ride to a mountain bike adventure over slick rock. But now I get to do the driving.

CHAPTER 12

"The Name I Call Myself When I Want Myself to Answer"

(from a poem written by Mbola Umoja)

"And then, who knows? Perhaps we will be taken in hand by certain memories as if by angels."
—MARGUERITE YOURCENAR

AN ICE CUBE MELTS, THEN EVAPORATES. Imagine you are the ice cube.

A drop of rain falls into the ocean and becomes part of a swelling wave. Imagine you are the raindrop. A hand grabs so tightly onto something for decades that it becomes numb, then finally, it just opens, releases with a sigh. Imagine you are the hand. Imagine the safest experience you could ever know.

I don't know how else to describe what it felt like to die. Some people reassure me that no explanation is possible, but many more keep begging me to tell them what it felt like—not what I learned or how I'm different as a result of the experience, but what it felt like. I know the experience defies expression in words, and I also know the telling of it can't really make a difference to anybody else. Yet still, twenty-five years later, I feel compelled to tell the story, including what I learned and how I'm different.

I was on an operating table in Boston. Or my body was. I heard the doctor yell to the nurse, "Damn! We lost her. Adrenaline stat!" I would have preferred hearing a Mozart concerto or Maya Angelou reciting "And Still I Rise" in a hot whisper in my ear. Even a cat purring would have been nice. But the doctor yelling was the last thing I heard. Then I melted and fell upward out of my body. It was a lot like falling in love, which I've always thought was a falling upward, falling out of fear.

While the doctor was swearing at the nurse, "I" was soaring past a thousand closing doors to what I had thought of as myself—all the nouns of identity disappeared in an instant, along with hope and horror. No more "mother," "sister," "friend." Just a soul in wonder.

There was no seeing or smelling or hearing. There was no more dissonance, no more fragmentation or feeling pulled apart. I was in complete resonance. What was left behind was my sweet old animal body that clamors for attention through my senses and the tickticktick that fettered me to a thousand notions of obligation.

People have asked me if I saw The Light. I have to tell the truth. My experience was more like bending toward light. It was like being stained with light.

And since every truth must balance with another, I also experienced a pervasive darkness. Not hellfire. But the awareness of how the soul's great capacity for love, the love that had been leaking out of my life for so long was excruciating. To know how incomplete my loving had been was agonizing—how I had limited it with all my stories that loving was a thing, a commodity I could "give" or not, had earned or not. The understanding of how much my son would suffer as a result of the limited ways I had realized my love for him was Hell enough.

There was a conversation, a dialogue without words, between my soul and the life I had lived. It took place in a complete white silence, and was more subtle than thought, more like the whispering between a tree and the wind blowing through it.

"Have you had enough joy?"

"Enough joy? I haven't even begun to live and now I've died!" (It's true, even in a sacred moment, I was complaining of not getting enough.)

"Well, what have you been you waiting for?"

(Imagine embarrassed sputtering here, as I became aware of how few of the moments I had been given had actually been experienced. It would be like giving someone a thousand dollars. They mindlessly throw 999 away and then complain they don't have enough.)

"What's unfinished for you to give?"

"What's unfinished for you to heal?"

"What's unfinished for you to learn?"

"What's unfinished for you to experience?"

What could I say? These questions did not demand answers. They required only that I open to them. I felt, in essence, my mind wanting to learn the way a seed wants to swell and sprout, my soul wanting to experience the way an apple branch wants to blossom, my heart wanting to give extravagantly the way that blossom wants to fruit.

Have you ever fallen asleep and then awakened with a start so that your body literally jumps? I fell back into my body, which was being wheeled on a gurney to the morgue. I would say now that I, who had never failed a test, flunked dying, except that I slammed into my body with the stunning awareness that death is not a failure.

I was so full of so much. I played in the sweet, simple ecstasy of breathing. It was as if I were some kind of silver fish whose inner eyelids had finally opened. I tried to tell the orderly who was pushing the gurney, but only bubbles came out of my mouth. I tried to explain to the doctor, who thought he had lost me, that nothing had been lost except my numbness and ignorance of what it truly means to be alive. I tried to tell David that if our hearts could begin to open to pain, grief, fear, joy, so would our lives.

I tried to tell my friends that we don't have to find our purpose, it is a current in our souls the way blood courses through our veins; that all we have to do is to let it find us. The orderly, the doctor, David, my friends, all responded as fish would if a scuba diver paddled down and told them they were swimming in something called water.

There is no end to this story. Ultimately, all I know is that we get to keep on practicing opening our hearts to the raw stuff of life that every human being experiences, the energy we label as fear, rage, pain, joy, and ecstasy. I know you can't get rid of any of it. You can only know it all with tenderness and honesty. I know we all suffer from a lack of compassion and mercy for ourselves and each other. I know I need to learn to observe with passion, to think with patience, and to live with care. I know we begin and end in authenticity, and in between, our task is to find ways to make that authenticity relevant to the world. I know there is nothing more precious that I can give than love. I know I forget all of this more often than I remember, and then I get to practice some more. And I will keep practicing, pressing vitality out of every last moment, until I die with a still-hungry heart.

Thomas Hardy once observed that your birthday exists in relation to another day, a day that is impossible to know: we pass silently, every year, over the anniversary of our death. How would it change you if you knew the date of when you were going to die? Would your priorities change? Pema Chödrön, author and teacher, describes how most of us go through life like people standing at the edge of the Grand Canyon with brown paper bags over our heads. Would the bag still be there if you knew your "death day" each year? How would you remove it?

Everything altered for me that day in the hospital, the way a tidal wave might alter your definition of a day at the beach forever. It was as if an invisible hand opened a rusty valve inside me. To everyone else, the world was just the same. To me, it was bathed in love, an unlimited source of energy that ran through me. It could never be used up or dried up. I can get in its way. I can shut off the valve, but the more of it I let flow, the more fulfilled I feel.

Part of what gets in our way, I think, is that we tend to think of ourselves so concretely, as if we are fixed in stone. Think of all the ways you stop yourself by saying something like, "Oh I couldn't do something like that. I'm the kind of person who...I'm too...I'm not...". What if you weren't so sure you knew who you were? What if deep inside, deeper than thought or guilt or worry, you told yourself you were a soul in wonder? How would that change the way you live your life?

Nothing was more resolved after I died. Nor is it now. I just fell in love with being alive. My mother used to wear girdles all the time, even when she slept. I know she'd hate my telling you this, but would allow it because it serves a good purpose. And that's what it's about—serving a good purpose. She got in the habit of wearing these tight rubber Playtex girdles when the style was that no woman should jiggle anyplace. I asked her a few weeks before she died why she still wore them, even under her nightgown. I suggested she could finally know what it would be like to be free at last, to let it all hang out, so to speak. She shook her head and said, "But Dawna, I wouldn't feel like me that way."

Don't disparage my mother. We all have stories about who we are that are exactly like my mother's girdle. And we wear them to bed as well. We cheat ourselves by identifying with a limited notion of who we are so we can fit in, belong to lives so much smaller than our souls long for us to be.

I have spoken about purpose to many CEOs of global corporations. When I inquire about theirs', they usually tell me about their "vision," and how it motivates them to work hard. Their eyes are like glazed doughnuts as they speak, their voices almost strangled, without resonance. I tell them about all the retired people who say they wish they had spent more time taking risks in relationships and work, more time searching for the big picture, more time making a real contribution to the world. I inquire about what feels choked off in them, what feels unfulfilled. Sometimes they clear their throats, look at their watches, and mention their next appointment. Usually, they fold their arms across their chests, straighten the papers on their desks, and tell me I'm too idealistic.

On rare and precious moments, someone will tell me about when he used to play the saxophone or when she used to dream about opening a halfway house for abused women or when he thought he could mentor boys in the inner city or when she was going to write a book about how she made it through her childhood. And they light up. There's no other way to describe what happens. Their cheeks flush, their bodies become animated, their voices are electric as they speak. For a moment, the clock stops ticking. Then they pause, shake themselves the way a dog does on a hot day after swimming in a cool lake, and they crawl back in their girdle, talk about money and time and reasons why not. "Well, Dr. Markova, I'm not the sort of person who could just.... I wouldn't feel like me that way." I watch heart failures as the clock begins to tick again.

My son once told me he didn't want to grow up to be a man because they all seemed like they were walking dead. I came back from being dead realizing we are totally free to live fully alive. Now. In this moment. Free to define ourselves. We are what we choose to be. I don't mean free to *have*. I mean free to *be*. I know

many among us don't have sufficient nourishment, space, education. But I also remember learning how Nelson Mandela sang of
freedom at the top of his lungs on a boat while being taken to
prison. And I remember the Jamaican angel who swept the floors
in a hospital and whispered words to me in the dark of the night
that changed everything: "You're more than your fear." I know
there are others among us who have more food than they can
ever eat, bigger houses than they can ever occupy, more education than they can ever use, and still they suffer from spiritual
insufficiency and lack of the kind of nourishment that a sense of
purpose brings. Most of us would never dare sing at the top of our
lungs on a boat for fear of being embarrassed!

Parker Palmer, author, mentor, and guide, wrote, "No punishment anyone might inflict on us could possibly be worse than the
punishment we inflict on ourselves by conspiring in our own
diminishment."

There are a few things I have done in the last fifty-seven years
that that I truly respect myself for—driving around the world
with a four-year-old for two years, writing some books about how
people can learn about how they learn, helping several children
who deserved a fine world know that they did, living with cancer
as a teacher, loving my mother through her death. The most
recent is coming to this cabin in the frozen dead of winter, and
stopping to listen to myself for half of a year, resting and receiv-
ing my own inner experience. I have learned to feel comfort in
my own silence, to listen until my heart knocks so loud I can hear
nothing else. I am learning to create the conditions where a sense
of purpose can arise. Where I can arise, all grumbly and confused.
All unknowing and skinless. Moving through the nerves of ques-

tions that cannot be answered. Living through the insecurity of misery rather than the misery of security. I begin to feel fully alive, to live by values that are truly mine, and to know again what really matters to me, in a rhythm that goes with the grain of my soul.

In West Africa, there is a saying that it's the heart that lets go and the hands that follow. I'm coming to understand that there is no such thing as *finding* one's purpose. It's about creating the conditions, for six months or six minutes, where your purpose can find you. It's not about asking what is the meaning of life, but rather asking what *your* life means. It's being willing to receive the truth of what you hear.

My friend, what would the conditions be that would allow your purpose to find you? What would have to happen so the meaning of your life really sustained you?

May we all release our hearts and allow our hands to follow.

IV

Living On Path:
Landscapes of the Spirit

"Purpose is the place where your deep gladness meets
the world's needs."

—FREDERICK BUECHNER

he light is rising out of the sweet darkness. It is
the day in which I celebrate the birth of my soul
into this body. It is a moment of perfect balance.
The sun is rising bronze in the east, the moon is
setting silver in the west, and a single coyote is piercing the
stillness with its howl. Dawn. The day after spring has been
born on the calendar, although judging by the five feet of
snow and the winds howling across the landscape, you'd be
hard pressed to tell from here. A friend, Juliy, gave me a bird's
nest as a gift. Neither of us has any idea what kind of bird created it, but it contains four tiny pinecones and is woven with
many moose hairs and pine needles. I am as thrilled with it as
I would have been with jewelry a year ago. I've been searching

for something in this frozen landscape with which to begin the last part of my journey. I imagine it speaking to me: *"I was a home, a sanctuary, a place to rest and nest the tiny carriers of seeds and possibilities which have broken open and flow out on their own. Now I have been abandoned, of necessity, so the next part of the cycle can emerge. If you try and hold onto me past my time I will crumble in your hands, because nothing can be permanent. All must change form in nature. It is time to release your dreams, in faith, to the world at large, and return."*

I'm not particularly happy about this. For the first time in my adult life, I have been nested in complete happiness in my own solitude, in this perfect world of my own making. But I notice that the sun now sets much further to my right each night and the chickadees coming to the feeder have a different call. I notice that when David or his wife Angie or Andy come to visit, I am fussier and fussier, wiping their muddy footprints after them, hanging their carelessly placed jackets, grumpy when they leave a book or magazine in a place other than where I think it belongs. The census taker leaves a trail of perfume behind and I open the windows so the cabin smells the way I like it to. I realize that I must control more and more to keep the world out. If I continue much longer like this, I will have made it into a perfect cage where only I can dwell. This cabin, like an identity, could become a prison.

It's time for me to move on. For while purpose has to be found in solitude, it has to be lived in community. Now, I am remembering a mysterious experience I had more than twenty-five years ago on my birthday on the other side of the Pacific Ocean. I spent several weeks meditating in a Buddhist monastery in northern Japan. I didn't really know much about meditation at the time, and none of the monks spoke English. I understood virtually nothing of what was going on, but it was so quiet, so peaceful there, that I was irresistibly drawn back, day after day. One morning as the monks and I were entering the meditation hall, the Roshi knelt by the door and bowed to each of us. Then he reached up and pressed his thumb onto each of our foreheads for a moment. When it was my turn, I smiled, bowed again and quietly took my place on a mat. Usually we meditators would be staring at a wall, but this day our cushions were arranged so that each of us sat around the periphery, our backs to the wall, facing the center.

After what seemed like an hour of following my breath, but was probably seven minutes, I found myself looking around at the meditating monks. I noticed that each of them had a different colored dot in the center of his forehead. That was what the Roshi had been doing. I forced my eyes back to the place on the tatami mat in front of me. My mind was racing. What did those dots mean? Did I have one? I must have one. The Roshi must have pressed one into my forehead when I was bowing. But why? And what color was mine?

Then I realized that I knew the color of the dot of every monk in the room and they knew mine, but no one knew their own. They must be as curious as I was as to the color of their dot. There were, of course, no mirrors. We were supposed to sit absolutely still. Even twitching or scratching was not allowed. I spent most of that session scheming on how to sneeze in such a way that I could surreptitiously scratch my forehead, getting just a bit of color on my nail. The gong sounded three times before I could work up the nerve. We all bowed to the center of the room, and then rose to leave, walking very slowly toward the door . . . one breath, one step.

The Roshi was waiting at the entrance. One by one, as we bowed, he smiled ever so slightly, reached up and, with a damp handkerchief, wiped off each dot. We smiled, bowed again and left, never to discover what every other person in that room could see as plainly as the forehead on the front of our face—the color of our dot.

What I didn't understand then, but am beginning to realize now, is that purpose is like those colored dots. We need each other to truly discover and enact it. Purpose is a constellation, not a destination. It is a pattern that helps us find our unique path to serving others, which, ultimately, is the only way we can serve ourselves. It's not a solution, a decision, or an event. It's not necessarily what we do for work, although work can be a vehicle for its expression. Rather, purpose is the current of a river hidden under the ice. It defines the energy with which we can commit to something, but not the outcome.

In the past months in this nest, I have come to understand that the pattern of my life, my purpose, is and has always been about four things: recognizing and leading forth the gifts within others and myself; cultivating wisdom; liberating the human spirit; and loving wide open. I've also learned that my life, to be fully lived, must weave together symbolic and intellectual ways of knowing into one tapestry.

As I begin to think about returning to the community to enact this, I realize that these four points of light could be realized in many ways. So how do I move forward toward them? I need some kind of navigational system that will help me find which actions and words will produce the results I truly want, a compass that will help me turn toward the light in order to create a future I can love and leave as a legacy.

I know that for me, each point on the compass will be an evocative question. In the past five months, I have come to recognize that the question I wake up with is the path I follow for the whole day . . . be it, "How will I ever get everything done?", which guarantees a blurred day spent in pursuit of crossing everything off the list so I can collapse into bed at the other end, or "How could I love this day as if I've never been hurt?", which results in living wide open.

Therefore, I need questions as my compass points, four questions that will be so easy to remember that even when I am most lost, I'll be able to recall and use them to align my decisions with my purpose.

At four in the morning, I sit bolt upright and watch my hand scribble out a word, LIVE. I realize that each letter represents a different question. I, who can never remember acronyms, who detests the secret and exclusive lettered languages that roll off the corporate tongues of every organization I have consulted to, has been given an acronym as an intuitive guidance system. It is a blossom in my mind. "L" stands for the question, "What do I love?" "I" represents "What are my inner gifts and talents?" "V" equals "What do I value?" And "E" means "What are the environments that bring out the best in me?" If I ask myself these four questions at any given intersection, I believe they will help me navigate on this mysterious journey of the soul.

I think now of the great and wise souls I have been fortunate to know. They seemed to navigate through life gracefully by consulting an inner homing device. These four questions formed a guidance system that drew them forward as if by a magnetic force. Their hearts, minds, and actions were congruently aligned, rather than having to push themselves ahead by what is commonly called "willpower."

At fifty-eight, I know I won't receive answers to these questions. I do trust, though, that if I stop and listen to the inner wisdom that is evoked in response to these questions, I'll discover a "thousand ways to kneel and kiss the earth." And I have faith that they will lead me to a path where "my deep gladness will meet the world's needs."

What do you truly love? To explore this question, it's helpful to go back to the seeds of your loving and ahead to the fruit you'd like it to bear in the world. Who taught you to see beauty in the world? Who believed in you, no matter what? Who was a great soul for you, an inspiring companion, who passed on to you a wonder and a love of some aspect of being alive.

CHAPTER 13

What Is Your Lineage and Legacy of Love?

"We don't inherit the world from our parents, we
borrow it from our children."
—GANDHI

WHEN I THINK OF MY GRANDMOTHER, EVEN TODAY, I smell bread. That's not exactly right. My head fills with the smell of yeast. All of my memories of her are coated with a mixture of sunlight and flour dust. I can mold her face in my mind, deep caves where her eyes peer out, high cheekbones defining a dignity nothing can ever trespass, a webbing of lifelines etching intricate designs in her skin. She was a tiny woman, shrunken, but her hands were large, timeless, the veins risen to the surface the way they do on maple leaves. Her long white fingers reminded me of tree roots plucked right out of the earth.

On Friday afternoons, I knelt on the floor next to the red oil-cloth-covered table in her kitchen watching those luxurious hands make bread for the Sabbath. Elbow deep in flour, she wove her wisdom into me while braiding the egg-yellow dough. I can't recall the sound of her voice. I'm not even sure if she spoke to me in English or Yiddish. What comes back is her warm palm resting on my forehead, as if transfusing a luminous stream of stories directly into my brain.

"People have energy which works in their lives the way this yeast does in the bread. At the very center, it pushes, stretches, demands to expand. If we don't give it the sweetness it needs to rise," her fingers tangled in the dough, "their souls get sick."
As she struggled to free her hands, the beautiful braid she had shaped was destroyed. She punched the dough flat again, flipped it, and lavishly sprinkled it and me with flour.

"Then we have to go back to the beginning and start all over with the kneading and rising."

Once I told her about a friend, Anthony Esposito, whose father owned a restaurant near my house. Tony's yeast, what he loved most of all, was giant stones. Grandma said it was a legacy from his grandfather, who used to be a mason in Italy. On weekends, he and the old man would go someplace in New Jersey and move big rocks around, crafting walls and stairways, steps and small bridges. She said his grandfather's legacy would enrich Tony's soul so he would be able to walk his own path. She told me that in some way my future would involve helping people learn and live from their hearts. I knew that the lineage of stories saturated with her love would be paving stones for my own path.

One Sunday, while she was brushing her silky white hair into a dense cloud, I ran my fingers over the carvings on top of a small camphor wood box that sat on her dresser, which had always fascinated me. Putting the brush down, she took the box from me and placed it in her own palm, opening and closing her hand several times. She said, "Hands, hearts, boxes—they all can be opened or closed. They're capable of both, yes?" I nodded and she stretched the box out to me. I very carefully pried the lid open with my thumbnail. Inside was a musty smell and a handful of dirt.

"Where did it come from, Grandma?"

"Home."

I looked around the apartment, but she shook her head and I knew then that she meant Russia.

"What's it for?"

She took a pinch of the dirt between her fingers and sifted it back into the box. Her voice got cobwebby as she said, "When I left the old country, I had to leave so much behind, so I took this handful of home with me. When we got off the boat on Ellis Island, I put a pinch under my feet to make a friend of the strange ground."

I don't know where she learned all she knew. She never went to school in her small Russian village. One day, when I asked, her cheeks got ironed flat and her long fingers traced the pale pink cameo pin she always wore on the collar of her black dress.

"It is the Sisterhood that passes their wisdom through me as if it were a ribbon carried by a needle. They come to me in my dreams. They'll leave ribbons for you too." I squeezed her hand, kissed her cheek, sweet with tiny golden hairs, and then proceeded to plague her with a mosquito swarm of questions. She said no more and never mentioned the Sisterhood again.

When I was twelve, my grandmother told me that I would have a son, and that there was a very important tradition I must remember to follow with him when he first began to read. Having a son seemed a ridiculous thing to think about back then, but traditions I liked. Traditions were candles, and feathers, and mysterious words and moving hands like flowers in the wind.

"When your son learns to read, the very first time, you must give him some honeycake, something sweet to eat. His mind will tie the two things together from that moment on—learning and sweetness."

I asked her if someone had given her something sweet to eat when she was a young reader. She pressed her lips tight. "I never learned to read. We had no books in my village, and besides I was a girl. Girls were for cooking and cleaning, not for books and learning. That's the way it was in the old country. That's why I wanted to leave. That, and the Cossacks and *pogroms.*"

I knew she didn't want to talk about those things. I wasn't sure what a pogrom actually was. I just knew it had to do with drunken soldiers and Jewish people being shot for fun late at night. I decided not to ask her any more, but I did want to know if she had given my father honeycake when he had learned to read. Her eyes got all red, as if they were bleeding, and her words got singsongy, as if she were mourning someone who had died.

"We were too poor for honey. Your grandfather was working in the sweatshop, and eight children were a lot of mouths to feed.

Your father had to drop out of school so he could work and help out. He never learned to read too well. It is the one thing I am ashamed of. That is why it is so important that you teach *your* son to love learning. Then it will be all right about your father. His seed will sprout through you and your child. You will both learn for me, for your father, for the children in the pogrom, for all of us. Remember about eating the honeycake so your minds will tie the two things together—learning and sweetness."

Fast forward twenty-five years. I dropped David off at college only eighty miles away, yet somehow it seemed as if I'd been preparing myself for the abysmal separation for years. Driving away, I wanted to reach out one last time and grab him, as if I were a small child trying to grasp a butterfly, but I knew I would end up with a handful of air. I felt random, random as grass trampled by feet racing somewhere else.

As he walked toward his freshman dorm, I saw him as a man who could handle himself in the stiffest wind, a man rooted and relevant, a man who had come through me, and was now unfurling into a life entirely of his own making.

Driving home, I found myself stroking moments of those eighteen years as if they were a scarf of precious silk, a fabric we had woven together. I searched for how I felt in my deepest place, the airy innocent place that knows mountains, woods, the earth and sky where he grew. I was trying to catch the meaning of my journey as a woman, a mother, trying to stir the sediment of my thoughts. I felt, instead, as if I were a thin empty tube with wind rushing through.

There were words I could not speak with him that day. I wanted to share the voice that had hidden behind scolding, prodding, nagging, arguments, complaints. How I wish I had had the courage, that last hour, to walk with him simple and open, arms entwined in the bronze explosion of the Vermont autumn! I wanted to find the words which would say it all, words that would make what I felt and what I wanted for him seem memorable and majestic, words that would melt us both into the moment. I didn't have the courage. I told myself I would feel awkward, he would be embarrassed. I spluttered trivialities in the vague spaces, gasping for words as if fighting for air.

I wanted to find words that would build a bridge between us in my mind. I wonder how he could possibly understand my journey—he, the erotic athlete of eighteen, me, the literate middle-aged woman. How could I cross that bridge and pass on what is so important to me?

My body has taught me that a terminal is a place where journeys begin as well as end. I have learned how holy time really is, how what's at issue is not how much we are given but how well we use what we have. I have discovered that it is possible to use time to press our spirits into footprints, fingerprints, mindprints that make a difference. I've learned that it is indeed possible to risk the immeasurable reach of which a human soul is capable in order to pass on what one loves to others.

Have I taught him any of that? Have I taught him anything about how to make a life? Have I taught him to ask himself over and over, "What do I need to do now to respect myself?" Have I taught him that without a passionate heartbeat, life is failed magic? I've dedicated myself to teaching other people the art of knowing themselves, of expanding their lives to risk their significance, but what have I taught my son?

Whatever I did or didn't teach him, it was time for him to hold his own in the unexpected. After so many years of shaping my living around his growing form, it was time for me to let go. Not disappear, just to release this thread I'd been weaving into the web of his life and begin again.

I had never wanted another child—what I had to give, he got. What I needed from a child, he gave. There was a looseness about everything for me that day, as if a new mind was implanted in the cavity of the old. For so many years, I told myself, "I must hold on for David's sake...." Now the word *must* had been erased and every act became a choice; a simpler and slower choice.

As I watched him walking toward his dorm, I saw that specialness he radiates, that directness, the straight elegance of a tree well planted in the right place. I liked who I had become as well, full, ripe, and reaching, the richness of earth well tended. I liked who each of us was becoming, and who each of us already was.

I prayed he would grow into a man who dared to risk his significance, who dared to learn to feel life—the sweetness, anguish, rapture, pain, all of it, all of him. I prayed he would learn to laugh his moments clean, and to yield always to love. I prayed I would learn to risk the passion of my own heartbeat, and live the mystery that was in my soul.

Living on purpose requires us to find what we love fiercely, give it all we've got, and then pass it on, as if it were a torch, to those who follow. My friend, Nancy Margulies, told me once about her grandfather, who explained to her that when a person dies, he or she has the opportunity to bequeath a legacy of love. He passed his love for Nancy on to her uncle, who expressed his own love for her plus that willed to him by her grandfather. Thus death never interrupts the shelter of love.

I'm thinking now of reading Rachel Carson's *A Sense of Wonder* when I became a first grade teacher. I felt the fire my grandmother had sparked in me reignite as if blown by a gentle wind by Carson's words: "If children are to keep alive their inborn sense of wonder, they need the companionship of at least one adult who can share it, discovering with them the joy, the excitement and mystery of the world we live in." Even now, more than three decades later, I gasp a little typing those words Carson wrote. Someone once told me every haiku has to have a gasp where God can enter. Every life, I think, has to have a gasp where God can enter. And every such gasp is a finger pointing at what you've spent your whole life loving.

My mind is wallpapered with reminders of this from people I've never met. I need the reminding because it's so easy to think my life is about making money or being productive or checking off everything on the list. Then I reach for a magazine and there's writer and activist bell hooks reminding me: "My students say 'We're tired of loving.' And I say, if you're tired of loving, then you haven't really been loving because when you are loving, you have more strength." And I remember. We grow stronger in the act of loving something. It sustains us. It generates energy. If I am depleted or feel as if I've failed, ultimately it is because I have not been living in service to what I love.

I listen to an audiotape while snowshoeing and anthropologist Angeles Arrien reminds me, "Think of all those who came before you whispering, 'Maybe this one will be the one. Maybe this one will be the one who breaks the old patterns of limitation. Maybe this one will be the one to live in service of what is true and beautiful.'" And I remember. I stand on my own two feet, but I do not stand alone. So many stand behind me. So many beings have sacrificed that I may stand here.

So many will come after us whose lives may be fuller richer, wider, and deeper because we risk living what we love. What no one loves vanishes. I cannot bear to think of the love of learning vanishing. Yet all around me I see that happening. Parents and teachers and politicians are talking about the fall of standardized test scores. Several million children in this country, including those in kindergarten, are being drugged because they learn differently or because they cannot pay attention to things that are irrelevant to them. Senior-level executives of global corporations that I coach walk around secretly feeling stupid or inarticulate or incompetent. Why are we not talking about what we can do to strengthen the love of learning?

Innovation is the trademark of our species. In order to become a doer and a maker, it is necessary that the mind's attention become enthralled by something. In order to become a maker of books, one must first fall in love with a book. Then another. We all learn through curiosity and attention, by confrontation and imitation. As children, our first experience of falling in love with a book or a stone or a river makes its way across the landscape of our still-forming mind and this can be the most important, emotive, influential experience to shape our destiny and purpose.

Too many children lose their love of learning shortly after they enter school. I cannot bear to see them sitting in doorways with hooded eyes, wondering if there really is a path ahead, wondering if there really are elders upon it. Yes, we are there, just ahead of you. The path is full of bends, potholes, distracting noises, and insults of all kinds, but there we are, just out of view, looking back, concerned for you.

What lights us up never truly abandons us. We abandon it. In a recent workshop, David and Angie interviewed people on video asking them how they would love to spend their lives if money were no object. Person after person "lit up," and later watched themselves do it on the replay. They lit up when they talked about teaching kids to love nature through trout fishing or helping women feel a sense of dignity in their work or teaching poetry to inner city boys. Then the inevitable "but . . ." would come and the abandonment of the light would begin again.

When I think about the stories of my grandmother and David that emerged when I asked the question, "What is my lineage and legacy of love?", the message is clear. Fostering the love of learning liberates my heart. It has been so for a long, long time in classrooms from kindergarten to graduate school, in corporate boardrooms, and migrant labor camps.

Now what? I still have no idea what I should be when I grow up. These two stories help me remember what kind of a future I need to co-create so that I can grow forward with passion. They help me remember what I need to dedicate my energy to so that my fire doesn't die a little each day. They help me liberate my heart and stay on the path of purpose.

What we love ennobles us. What no one loves vanishes. Kurt Wright, a consultant, said that the purpose of life "is to learn to love, to discover just how much of God's love each of us can allow to flow through with no interference on our part." I turn again to you, dear reader. What do you love so much that in the doing of it you find a kind of grace in the world? Who stands behind you in this lineage? Who stands in front of you, waiting for your legacy?

May we remember those who passed on to us the seeds of their dreams so that we might grow. May we live our dreams with dignity so that we may pass them on to those who turn to us for their future.

What are your inner gifts and talents? Most of us are reasonably articulate about our deficits and weaknesses—how many we got wrong on our spelling tests, how many things we have failed to accomplish during any given day. We become fluent at explaining our incompetencies, but look straight at our gifts and talents and then mutter, "Oh, that old thing?" This leaves us awkward and confused about how to bring our assets and resources to the rest of the community. Too many of us believe we don't matter, and that what we do doesn't really make a difference.

CHAPTER 14

What Have I Been Given with Which to Give?

"While you have a thing it can be taken from you . . .
but when you give it, no robber can take it from
you. It will be yours always."
—JAMES JOYCE

ONCE I SAW AN AD IN THE BACK PAGES OF THE SUNDAY *New York Times* magazine section for a green plastic safe that was shaped to look and feel exactly like a moldy cabbage. You didn't need a combination or key. You held it in just the right way, it split open so you could hide your jewels inside, and then slipped it into the hydrator of your refrigerator. The idea was that even if a thief was to open your refrigerator, looking for something precious, or happened to be hungry in the middle of breaking and entering, she or he would never think to open the vegetable drawer. (Who eats vegetables while committing Grand Theft?) Even, if by some chance, that drawer was opened, who would want to touch, let alone eat, a slimy, moldy cabbage? And if a miracle should occur and the thief, desperately ravenous, did take it out, he or she would never have the patience to hold it just so until the secret clasp could be found that would open it to reveal the inner treasure.

I happen to think that God has a remarkable sense of humor and hides our most precious gifts and talents inside us in some place like the moldy cabbage, so that we really have to be willing to wonder, to re-spect (literally, to look at again) that which we have assumed was "that old thing" hanging out in a dark storage drawer of our minds.

I think in stories. You may have guessed. Some people think in songs. Some people think in logical dots and details. Some in poems. Some, like the man I'm going to tell you about in this story, think in formulas. I always considered my stories to be my moldy cabbage. First of all, they got me into a lot of trouble growing up. My very precise and grounded sister said I was lying. My parents said I exaggerated. My Girl Scout leader, before kicking me out of the troop, said I had an overactive imagination. My graduate advisor told me I was being overly dramatic and needed to learn to think in a straight line instead of interwoven loops and spirals.

Then I studied the work of Milton Erickson, which taught me more than anything else to rest in the place where the stories were born. Milton also thought in the language of stories. He helped me trust when stories just unfurled from my mind and dropped into my ears, without worrying about whether they were accurate or where they came from. Now, when I'm working with someone who is stuck or confused, I just stop, assume they need a story, and listen for one. Which is what happened when I was sitting with the man I told you about, whose mind thinks in chemical formulas.

When I first met him at a conference, he looked both wealthy and empty: haunted eyes that were the color of overturned earth, arms tightly bound across a sunken chest, shoulders that sloped downward as if he were carrying something too heavy on his back. He told me he was born in South America and was the first one in his family to go to college. He had a doctorate in chemistry and had progressed up the ladder to the point where he was the chief administrator of a large chemical company. He said he lived in a world of paper and numbers and felt dead inside, even though people described him as a grand success and he made lots of money. As I listened to him speak, I could feel no burning in him—all smoke but no fire.

He said he felt lost, confused, unsure of which way to go. The perfect opportunity, I thought, for his mind to rest and wonder. But he told me he hadn't rested or paid any real attention to his inner world since he had been divorced thirteen years before and took some time off. So I asked him to tell me two stories about times when he had been at his best and felt fulfilled.

He began with an explanation of why he felt so empty. But I was rude and interrupted. I told him I needed to help him find the formula for his pattern of filling up and spilling over, not the reasons for his emptiness. Finally, he let his heart speak. He told me of a time he had traveled to a former Communist country and toured around many of their weapons plants. He spoke of how he talked to the chemists there and helped them see how they could use their gifts to discover new medicines that would heal, instead of creating weapons that would destroy. As the story unfolded of how he helped them regain their lost dignity, his energy ignited, his eyes flashed, and I melted like butter on warm bread.

Then he told me about how filled up he felt when he came home from work and his children jumped all over him and covered him with kisses. He just lay on his back, doing nothing, producing nothing, and they lavished him with love and levity. Suddenly, he switched stories midstream, as if doing a turn in a tango. A few months before, there had been a hurricane in his country and he went out in the streets looking for ways to help people. "I just did simple things for complete strangers—boarded up windows, carried children to dry ground, but I felt so content helping them reclaim what had been lost." His voice grew soft as a breeze.

And then it happened. A story dropped into my left ear. It unraveled easily. "I'm thinking about something I heard recently," I said. "There was a little church in a plaza called Santa Rosa. One Sunday morning, as the congregation filed in, there was a loud intake of breath. The statue of Jesus stood in the corner as usual, but vandals had entered the chapel and broken off its hands. After Mass, the priest organized a committee of parishioners to investigate the crime and buy another statue.

"The following Sunday, as the congregation filed in for Mass, there was another loud intake of breath. This time, a sign was hanging around the statue's neck. It was carefully hand-lettered and read: 'I have no hands but yours.'"

The chemist's eyes filled with tears that slowly traced paths down his brown cheeks. I sat and breathed with him until he spoke, "You could not have known."

He shook his head and looked up at me. "When I was young, my family attended that tiny church in Santa Rosa. I was an altar boy there. Each Sunday, I would commit to be Jesus' hands. I left that little chapel feeling so full, so committed to helping people any way I could." He reached out to grab my hands. "I have gotten so busy with what I thought were important things, that I overlooked the most important gift I can bring. As long as I am helping people in some real way to regain their sense of dignity, I can serve as His hands. Nothing else really matters, does it?"

Now, I had never heard of Santa Rosa and what does a Jewish girl from Brooklyn know about Jesus' hands? But the rapture in his dark eyes was jewel enough for me.

How can you or I create a relationship between our gifts and the community that needs them? Immediately, this question calls up an image in my mind. It is of a poster I once saw of Vedran Smailovic, a brilliant cellist from Sarajevo, serenading crowds of people who stood around him in the ruins of the national library. During the war, he played every day at four in the afternoon, no matter what, so the people never lost heart.

That image is followed by an interview I heard last night on NPR with the man from Tennessee who started Habitat for Humanity, a worldwide organization that builds houses with and for people who could otherwise never afford a dwelling of their own. He had been a builder and real estate developer who, upon retirement, searched for some way to use his gifts. He told of how hundreds of thousands of houses have now been built around the world by people like you and me joining with the people who would inhabit them. He described how the process was so fulfilling that it brought most people involved to the joyous tears that come when we know we are serving others from our hearts.

Stories are flying by now like newspapers in a wind. One of my gifts is being a possibilist. In other words, when most people see deficits, I tend to look on the other side of the tapestry and see assets. Here's an example. I always wanted to be part of a gang when I was a young. I studied them carefully ... how the kids talked and dressed and strutted around. I could have written a book on the subject of gangs and how they can serve adolescents' needs. But kids who could write books are usually not the kids invited to join gangs.

After helping coedit two books, *Random Acts of Kindness*™ and *Kids' Random Acts of Kindness*™, I had an idea that I shared with a friend, Denys, who was a social worker. What if we helped *start* gangs in the inner city for young kids, gangs that had handshakes, colors, rap songs—all the indicators that help teenagers know they belong to a tribe, and matter? But these gangs would be dedicated to doing random acts of kindness to balance out the random acts of violence that other gangs were perpetrating. What if we could get them just as much publicity as the other gangs? Denys, who is also a renegade at heart, leapt into action. He brought Andy and me to Pittsburgh to help, and then he took over. There are now RAOK gangs in full swing all over the city. These stories remind me that using one's gifts in service to the community is not necessarily about what job we have or what we do for money. It is about our profession—how we use what we are given to profess our faith.

All of this thinking about gifts brings me to a mystery, a riddle. It brings me to what Parker Palmer calls "the theory of limits." He puts it this way: "There is as much guidance in what does not and cannot happen in my life as in what does." He says we burn out not by giving away too much, as most of us think, but by trying to give what we don't possess. In other words, our limitations as well as our gifts are great indicators of where and how we should be living our purpose. None of us can do everything—the skill is in knowing how to capitalize on our strengths and allow our limitations to indicate what *not* to give.

A friend of mine, Delia, is highly intuitive, sensitive to environments, and wanders and wonders through her life like a precious butterfly. She went to graduate school to get her MBA because people told her it would help her "come down to earth." Somehow, she managed the three years required. Antidepressants helped. She went through alternating waves of hating her professors and hating herself. She finally liberated herself from both the medication and the incarceration. She now is a gifted therapist and artist working with corporate executives who thrive in an environment that was her limitation.

Think of petting a cat against the way its fur naturally grows. Better yet, think of trying to create a beautiful piece of furniture by going against the grain of the wood.

When the chemist, the man I spoke of at the beginning of this chapter, was working only in a world of paper, he was going against his own grain. He was interfering with the flow of love trying to come through him.

I have struggled with defiance my whole life. I wanted desperately to fit in someplace, so I tried to mold myself into a submissive, "good" member of society. But, inevitably, the life-force within me wilted, and I'd be fighting some authority figure. If I couldn't find a boss, I'd create one just so I had somebody to push against. Then I'd feel ashamed, an outcast, because I was abnormal, too stubborn to commit. What I learned from Parker is that we cannot all do everything. It is not in the nature of every seed to be an oak tree, an eggplant, and a gladiolus. It is not in my nature to bloom within a greenhouse. I am a wildflower, a weed perhaps. I need open and untamed spaces to sprout. I need to ask the questions and think the thoughts that others overlook. Parker calls himself an "educator-at-large." In hearing that, finally I recognize a profession to which I can aspire. Finally I know the significant soil in which my gifts can blossom, and finally, I have found a gang where I can belong.

The blessing of understanding our limitations as well as our gifts is that we realize we need each other. We need people who can flourish within institutions as well as outside of then. We need people who can think in formulas and we need people who can think in stories. We need people who can play a cello in the midst of heartache and we need people who can paint the posters that remind the rest of us it is possible. Ultimately, we have no choice. We need each other.

And we need you, my friend, to ask yourself, kindly, fervently, "What have I been given with which to give? Where do my talents and the needs of the world intersect?"

May all who are different bring their unique gifts to the community and know they belong.

What really matters to you? Your values are an activating intelligence in your life, guiding you toward the noble tasks that are yours alone to do. There are moments in all of our lives that reveal these values. Their significance lies not only in what meaning we make of them, but also what we allow those moments to make of us.

CHAPTER 15

What Are You Serving?

"If we are really honest with ourselves, we must admit that our lives are all that really belong to us, so it is how we use our lives that determines what kind of persons we are. And it is my deepest belief that only by giving our lives do we find life. I am convinced that the truest act of courage, the strongest act of humanity is to sacrifice ourselves for something higher—that which we believe in and love deeply."
—CESAR CHAVEZ

I WONDER WHY IT IS THAT WE SO OFTEN imprison ourselves in the opinions of other people. There can be no punishment worse than conspiring in our own diminishment. Yet liberation, ultimately, is a solitary and stubborn affair, requiring old-fashioned cussedness and much rehearsal. I practiced quitting smoking, for instance, thirty-seven times. People told me I had an addictive nature and my "won't" power was stronger than my "will" power. It was true— I told myself, "I won't give up the 'present' of forty cigarettes a day," until I discovered something that I wanted even more—the present and frequent experience of freedom in my life.

When I was eight years old, I was told by a doctor that I was "constitutionally inadequate," which meant that my physical structure was somehow not enough to do what it was supposed to do in order for me to be a normal member of the human race. This was confirmed and repeated over the years by physical education teachers, camp counselors, adolescent boyfriends, and the merciless downpour of a Barbie Doll culture. My body was a mistake in which I was imprisoned for the rest of my life. The bars were reinforced by my father's beatings, by the man who raped me at fifteen, and by my first husband's psychiatrist, who insisted I was frigid, a "cold fish," incapable of experiencing pleasure in my body.

I went through five miscarriages, the murmur of "constitutionally inadequate" hissing in my ears, confirming that my body had failed again. Finally the doctor said I had better stop trying. That was too much. Finally my "won't power" rose on my own behalf—I was not going to allow anybody to steal my hope. No one had the right to take away my will to foster life. No one.

My sixth pregnancy was glorious, shining, nothing less than a wondrous miracle. My body did everything it was supposed to do perfectly. When I finally went into labor on exactly the day predicted, I remembered my grandmother telling me that some women experienced a "walking labor." My body followed her call—I went through most of labor walking around, cleaning the refrigerator, feeding our cat, ironing underwear. By the time I reached the hospital, I was five centimeters dilated and experiencing nothing more intense than menstrual cramps. The white-coated volunteer at the registration desk sat me in a wheelchair and calmly delivered me to the maternity floor. I remember thinking that the intern looked like the gentle television doctor, Dr. Kildare.

When he spread my legs to examine me, however, any resemblance of calm vanished. He started shouting and rushing. His feet pounded down the antiseptic hallway, propelling the gurney to the delivery room. I remember feeling quite delighted with myself, realizing that I was too far along to have to be shaved or suffer through an enema.

The double doors exploded open. The intern slid me over onto the delivery table and ordered me to pant until my obstetrician, who had just begun to scrub up, arrived. As soon he left, I, defiantly followed my body's urge, pulled myself up into a squatting position, and began to push.

Dr. Epstein, the obstetrician I'd chosen for his brown cocker spaniel eyes and clean slim hands, rushed into the delivery room. His soft voice tried to persuade me to slow down. "Not so fast, not so fast, Dawna."

But people have been telling me that my whole life. Going fast was the best way I knew to avoid pain. Talk fast enough and you won't even notice your feelings of terror. Think fast enough and you won't even notice a thousand small violations being done to you.

No matter how fast I was breathing as I squatted on the delivery table that day, I could not avoid the intensity of the pain. After one hour I was sure everyone had been right, and I was not up to the task. By that time, Dr. Epstein and the nurse had me strapped down and scissored open. My mind was completely ready to give up and get out of there as fast as possible. To my dismay, my body made it clear this was not an option. I remember shouting at Dr. Epstein, "I can't. I just can't. You don't understand. I'm not strong enough to do this. *You* do it."

He kept telling me to push, push. Finally, I looked up into that blinding white glass eye of an operating room light and surrendered. What happened next was an astonishment that has sustained me ever since. It was as if I rose upward while bearing down. My grandmother's voice called to me saying, *"They'll all tell you it's painful, that you're not strong enough. Don't you believe them. It's just hard work, like pushing a piano uphill. And you can do it. You can do it because you're not alone. Millions of women throughout time have done this and they will help you. Your body will know what to do. Remember, you're not alone."*

In that moment, I felt them surrounding me. All those women circling me, lifting me, reaching out to and for me with hidden hands, midwifing the baby through my body, through the doorway into this life. There were no lines dividing them from me, or me from the force of life itself. I began to laugh in a way I never had before. It was as if a green Niagara Falls spilled through me. No matter how much work it was, I knew I wanted this baby to be welcomed into a world of laughter, a world of joy. I knew he had a gift to bring to all of us and I was to help midwife it.

Dr. Epstein's voice came to me. "It's over now, Dawna, easy now, easy. Your son is born and he is perfect."

My son? I knew in the buoyant moment he placed that miraculous lump of life in my arms that Dr. Epstein was wrong. This jewel of my flesh was not *my* son. He was a wonder of wholeness, a miracle entire unto himself. And I knew that looking at David, holding him, witnessing his unfurling, would be an ever-present reminder that my body was enough. I knew I was enough. I knew I belonged. David connected me to the past, to all the women who have ever had children, and wove me into the future. I was now connected by, and committed to, the wild, valorous, and amazing web of life.

One very early morning thirty-two years later, I sat sipping a cup of steaming tea at my desk in this cabin, feeling like I was floating in a meaning void. I was wondering what really mattered to me, if anything still wanted to be birthed through me. I began to stare out the window, something my parents had routinely interrupted, telling me I was wasting time. (Little did I know then that to write, to think thoughts all the way down to the place where they thud into the fertile soil of your intuitive mind, you have to stare out the window.)

A thirty-mile-an-hour wind was sculpting the snow into one new landscape after another. As I put my cup down on the glass table next to me, I noticed a very tiny spider spinning a web between the two legs of the chair I was sitting on. The rising sun pouring in the window had made the web visible. As I watched, fascinated, my mind grabbed the thought like a strand and swung back to another spider web, to a field of webs actually, that I saw on a very early morning in a retreat center near Madison, Wisconsin. They were the creation of wolf spiders, I found out, who spun their webs between two blades of grass, which made them very flexible in strong winds. I never would have seen them except for the dew that clung to the strands and the dawn's light.

The Native peoples tell a story about Spider Woman who emerges in times of powerful transition, pulling apart the threads that formed the old world and spinning stories that will bring new forms into existence. I think of her as the part in each of us that cares deeply about what really matters, the part that insists we live our values rather than just talk about them. Lived values are like webs, strung between the events and experiences, the great and ordinary people of our daily existence. In the morning light, I realized how many women have been midwives of the possible for me, how many men have been the drops of dew clinging to those strands, how many hidden hands have reached out to me across dark abysses.

The Mothers of the Plaza de Mayo in Argentina twenty years ago form a strand in my mind. Do you remember the fourteen of them, walking in slow, fierce, silent circles with white scarves around their heads, braving night sticks and police dogs as they protested the disappearance of their children? I remember the great Argentinean poet Pablo Neruda saying, "The mothers are out. The military has already lost." I understood then that life is not a spectator sport, that we are not its victims, but its cocreators. I also understood that children call us forth into what Martin Luther King, Jr., named "soul force," the strength of the heart to love even in the face of the most difficult circumstances.

Spider Woman now spins a strand in my mind to an engineer who was responsible for stewarding a five-year process to create a copy machine in which every part was recyclable. She had to fight "the powers that be" long and hard in order to birth this machine and prove it was possible to create something that would not contribute to the waste that is suffocating our world. When somebody visited the factory that was now producing these machines, he was stunned at what she had accomplished and asked, "Who are you to take such a stand?" She was quiet for a long time, cleared her throat, and then replied in a determined voice, "I'm a mother."

Another strand unwinds from Spider Woman's belly and connects my mind to the poet Maya Angelou. She was supposed to give the keynote speech at a conference I attended in Orlando, but she was ill, so the organizers videotaped her in her home. At the conference, she was projected across time and space onto a screen so big that there was nothing else in the darkened auditorium except her flashing black eyes and bittersweet chocolate voice: "Who and what are you serving?" In that moment, not one of the thousand of us in the room could luxuriate any longer in the illusion that we were just bystanders.

Now, Spider Woman attaches my mind to a hose, an ordinary, garden-variety hose. If purpose is like a river, an energy similar to water, then think of your capacity as if it were a hose, and your mind a nozzle to direct the flow of energy. If we feel empty and focus on filling ourselves up to get satisfaction, it is like trying to get water from others and put it into the nozzle. We forget that the source of the energy, purpose, is from a spring larger than we can even imagine, and that it is by spilling over, ultimately that we are the most fulfilled. Thus, when I am empty and think I need to feel loved, for instance, what I really need may be to express love out into the world in some way that is meaningful to me.

In Hebrew there is a wonderful phrase, *tikkum olam*. It means "repairer of the world's soul," and as I understand the story from which the phrase comes, every day the world's soul becomes unraveled in some way. Each of us is a mender of it, as if we all hold, with both hands, the edge of a blanket that covers the world. It is each of our responsibilities to repair our edge of the blanket as far as we can reach.

What do all of these story strands say about my values and what matters to me now? Like the wolf spider swinging invisibly between two blades of grass, I am aware how important wholeness is to me, how important bridging certain polarities has been for me during the past five years—between the corporate world and the academic world, between the analytic mind and the intuitive, between active ways of knowing and receptive, between stimulation and nourishment, between work and family. I realize how adamantly I have refused to name that gap as the distance between the masculine and the feminine. It is so obvious to me that our burning comes from the same lamp—the cultivation of wisdom—so often dimmed in our culture.

Spider Woman wonders, "What if...?" What if I could travel back and forth with grace and ease between inner and outer, between analytic and intuitive? What if I could help the world to conspire in the expansion of children's gifts rather than diminishing them by deficit labeling and medication because they learn differently? What if I could weave a web between women of influence in the world so the organizations they lead could create the conditions that foster their unique way of knowing?

I don't know how these all "fit" into one web, but I trust I can spin a thread between the present moment and a possible future for my son and granddaughter. I know that midwifing the intuitive and cultivating inner wisdom are the values that call me forth, burning. I also know that, as at David's birth, I am not alone. There are women around the world who will help. There are men who are struggling to live from their hearts as well as their minds, who search for ways to enhance the relationship between their gladness and the world's needs.

And you, dear reader? What web has Spider Woman been weaving in your life? What values are at your core? Where do you take a stand? Who are you to take that stand? Where are you willing to risk your significance?

May we all find the courage to offer ourselves fully to what has heart and meaning for us.

What are the environments, the ways of working, and who are the people that bring out the best in you? As a result of the fragmentation most of us have experienced, we have become more convinced of our separation than our connection. Thus, we don't really consider that the environment in which we work can determine whether or not it is ever possible for us to bring our gifts to the community.

CHAPTER 16

Where Am I Meant to Be Shining?

(adapted from *Don't Call It Night* by Amos Oz)

"Is the life I'm living the life that wants to live in me?"
—PARKER PALMER

I AM IN A GROUP LISTENING TO DEE HOCK, founder of the Visa Corporation, in Wellington, New Zealand. He stands in the center of a circle of native Maori people and business leaders, saying, "It doesn't matter so much who we have been to each other historically. The only questions that really matter are, 'Who are you becoming?' and 'What kind of a world are we leaving for all of our grandchildren?'" His words move like a fire across all of our hearts. Silence gathers in the room and hovers. I wonder, How do I even dare begin to think about these questions without feeling despair?

Two years later, I am walking along the ocean's edge at dawn, in Santa Barbara, California. I am walking behind Thich Nhat Hanh, a Vietnamese teacher, poet, and monk. He wears a loose brown jacket and pants, with a brown knitted hat pulled down over his teacup ears. A thousand others walk behind him, a herd of strangers when we start, a flock that fans out slowly along the sandy cliffs, an undulating school, following this one small man who breathes in rhythm with the ocean, in and out, where the shoreline meets the sea.

Each of his feet, encased in wooden-soled clogs, presses slowly into the wet sand of the beach, synchronized with both the waves and his breath, leaving momentary emblems of his presence. Then they are washed away.

Joggers bounce by in the opposite direction, staring. Seaweed tangles around my ankles. Black globs of oil wash ashore from the derricks on the horizon. Two thousand feet follow his, in no obvious order, all in rhyme with breath and tide.

I breathe to carry myself across the void that I so meticulously avoid, the tiny black holes in my mind where there is nothing. No place to go, nothing to do, to have, or to be.

Someone brings a small brass bell out of a pocket and strikes it gently. He stops. We all stop. I feel something pulsing in both feet. Blood. The river of my life pouring into the ocean. My periphery widens, the emptiness opens. I settle down into myself.

And it is enough. The seaweed, the runners, the seagulls floating by, the thousand people standing still on a beach in Santa

Barbara, breathing with a small man dressed in brown, breathing with the waves, under the blue-gray sky that holds the clouds, the mind that holds the thoughts, that holds us all, that holds me.

Hours later, while we sit listening to him in a drafty sports arena, he says, "I walk for you. Every day. When you are lost in chaos or despair, I will be walking in peace and harmony some place in the world. You can know that I am walking for you."

Meanwhile, the other monks and nuns placed small turquoise paper circles in our sandals that were lined up neatly outside. Each one said the same thing: "I walk for you."

I'm sure he is walking for me now, months later, as I sit rocking in this cabin, thinking about what kind of environment I need in order to return to the world of needs and demands without losing myself or my sense of purpose. What are the conditions that will help me to be as I was with those thousand people, a part of the community, and yet apart from the community? How do I stay true to myself? How do I stay aligned with the natural rhythms that nurture my body and soul? How do I help create a community of connection rather than fragmentation? How do I live in a way that brings out the best of who I am?

I float in the space between my questions. I know they can't be answered. I need to ask them, again and again, to use them to find my way on this path. I rock in wonder at this sweet and peaceful moment when the aspen trees all around me, blaze green-gold in the late afternoon light. They are such a wonder, connected by invisible roots, yet separate as they emerge from the soil, reaching, thrusting themselves into this impossibly wide blue-violet sky that holds everything in its embrace.

I rock here thinking of the invisible roots that connect me

even now, when I am alone, to a community larger than I can even imagine. The deeper I go into myself, the more interconnected I realize I really am. I rock in the peace of this moment for who I have been when life was only a long trail of tears, and for who I will be again when I forget what really matters. I rock for my son and the daughter of my heart. I rock for my grandmother, for my adopted granddaughter, for the mother in China who had to abandon her. I rock for Dee's grandchildren. I rock for my father who beat me. And I rock for my husband who has such exquisitely clean hands. I rock in the wide serenity of this clear afternoon for all who are in offices under fluorescent lights, tangled in traffic, or trapped in the agony of conflict. I rock for those of us entombed in numbness and despair.

If you took a blue spruce tree and planted it in the desert, it would quickly perish. How do we forget that we too are living systems, and each of us has unique environments, needs, and conditions within which we flourish or wither?

Recently I read of an experiment where a scientist raised some baby fish in a small glass tank, which was inside a larger tank that held adult fish. The little fish in the smaller tank could see the fish in the larger tank, but because of the glass barrier they could not swim out. Once the small fish had grown up, the researcher removed the glass walls of the small tank so that they could swim out. But instead they stopped at the exact place that used to be their walls. The habit and memory of the edge of their world was more real to them than the freedom that was possible now that the glass had been removed.

Like these fish, we've been accustomed to swimming in a limited environment, convinced that this is the only way we can survive. We don't have to accept the environments that have been given to us, however. We can give ourselves much more space to expand by asking what are the conditions that bring out the best in us.

Since we can only feel fulfilled when we are sharing our gifts in community, purpose insists that we be connected to both the interior and the exterior world. But, but, but ... how can this be possible? How can we support both our inner and outer lives? For so many of us, living with an external orientation has become a deeply ingrained habit. Our culture insists we compartmentalize our inner life, wall it off behind the technical skills necessary to manage "out there."

But, as Annie Dillard writes, "If you go far enough inward, you find 'the unified field,' our complex and inexplicable caring for each other and for our life together." On the beach in Santa Barbara, I found this to be more than some abstract idea. Turning inward, I found myself in a place that was beyond ego, beyond even the notion of "I." I found myself caring and connected to what Parker Palmer calls "the community we share beneath the broken surface of our lives."

What are the living conditions that empower us instead of imprison us? What are the "no matter whats" in our environment that we need in order to grow an authentic and generous life? What I share here now is as illustration, since it is only true for me. Because we are unique living systems, each of us has a unique environment in which we flourish. It is my hope that reading my "no matter whats" will help you tap into your own:

No matter what, I need to be living and working in a spacious natural environment that encourages me to expand. Since my habit is to contract in uncertainty, and since uncertainty is the soup of modern life, I can most easily remind myself to expand when I am surrounded by a wide horizon.

No matter what, I need to be moving at a rhythm that allows my body, soul, and heart to be in alignment.

No matter what, I need to work both as a part of and apart from the larger community. I need to work with the family of my heart and body. Work has divided me from them for so many years. Now I need work to unify us, to join us in the task of bringing shining and useful things to the larger community.

No matter what, I need a balance of language, images, and lavish silence, so I can be guided by the inner voice of my intuitive mind and balance insight and outreach. I need the space to think thoughts all the way through until they open into wonder.

No matter what, I need a human atmosphere that constantly challenges me to be sane, thoughtful, wholesome, and present in the moment. If I am not present, there can be no meaning. If I am, everything I do has meaning.

No matter what, I need to be living and working in an environment that stimulates, pleases, and enlivens my physical being.

No matter what, I need to work in a climate that is interdependent, where the norm encourages us to use each other's strengths so no one of us has to carry more than our part.

And lastly, no matter what, I need to work in a creative atmosphere that encourages me to let die what is finished and foster new life that is trying to emerge.

Now it's your turn, dear reader. What are the influences, activities, and people that cause you to shine? What is a metaphor you would use to describe the environment that fosters your wisdom and helps you to bring your gifts out to the rest of us who are waiting for them? What are the circumstances? Are you at your best inside of an organization or outside or with one foot in and one foot out? Do you light up working alone, in a team, or both? Leading, following, or both?

May we all find the soil in which the seeds of our dreams can germinate into lives that are free of the limitations of our previous history, lives that are full and warm and rich with amazement.

Epilogue

The Seasons of Renewal: A Living Landscape

"Self-care is never a selfish act—it is simply good
stewardship of the only gift I have, the gift I was put
on earth to offer to others. Anytime we can listen to
true self, and give it the care it requires, we do so
not only for ourselves, but for the many others
whose lives we touch."

—PARKER PALMER

I began this retreat reading Anne Morrow Lindbergh,
and as I follow it to completion, the questions she
asked on her search for meaning echo in the canyons
of my bones: "When I go back, will I be submerged
again, not only by centrifugal activities, but by too many centripetal ones? Not only by too many distractions but by too
many opportunities?... The multiplicity of the world will
crowd in on me again with its false sense of values. Values

weighed in quantity not quality; in words not in thoughts; in acquisitiveness not in beauty. How shall I resist the onslaught?"

And I echo back to her words, how shall I achieve balance? The world at large cannot replace the largeness of my own individuality. The "there and then" of the future cannot be a substitute for the "here and now" of the present.

My mind catapults to the first time I heard the phrase "Be Here Now," spoken by Ram Dass. A few months ago, I heard him again. This time, he was rolled on stage in a wheelchair after several years of rehabilitation from a stroke. His words were halting, yet as profoundly awakening as they had been for me twenty-five years earlier: "I've died and been reborn so many times in this life. In the '50s, I was a professor at Harvard and then I died from that and I became, with Timothy Leary, part of the 'turn on, tune in, and drop out' messianic whatever-it-was in the '60s. This was a whole different incarnation. And then that ended. I went to India and I came back with beads, a long beard, and white robe, Baba Ram Dass, a spiritual teacher, more or less an Indian guru. But then I died from that. In the late '70s and '80s it was the Seva Foundation: hospitals in Nepal, India, and Guatemala, a work of service. And then this stroke happened. If I think back to my old life—my golf clubs in the closet, my cello in the living room—if I think that I'm the person who played music on that cello, I would really suffer and be so sorry for myself. But I'm not him. He died. Now I've been born again into this disabled body. This is who I am now. You have to take the curriculum as it comes to you."

My father would never have understood. He would have said that this poor man couldn't make up his mind what he wanted to be when he grew up. But my father grew up in a different time, a time when the predominant cultural myth was that of the machine, the good old steady machine of which people were the gears. They received a pattern at birth that told them who they were. If they worked hard enough, things got better and better until their parts wore out. And then they were given another machine, a gold watch, and then they died, a company man.

I remember listening to the big mahogany radio in the living room when I was very little and my father was still in his prime. We heard that a man named Edwin Hubble had developed a machine, a huge microscope, and through it he saw that there was another galaxy besides the Milky Way. It was called Andromeda. We were both stunned beyond anything we could imagine.

Now the Hubble telescope has seen billions of galaxies. Nobody knows where they came from. It's a mystery. But our guiding metaphor is changing. We know we belong to much larger worlds than we can imagine. We know now that we are not replaceable parts of a machine. We know we are unique living systems, interconnected and interdependent with other living systems. We know, as living systems, that everything within us is capable of decay—matter, beliefs, passion—and we know that anything capable of decay is also capable of renewal and regeneration.

This is more than an enabling fiction. It brings both challenge and comfort. There's no part of creation that does not go through a cycle of growth, falling away, disappearing and reemerging. Think of a tree. Or the moon. Why should humans be the one aspect of life that is exempt from this cycle? Our pulse beats in varying rhythms, as all of nature's does. Why then do we move at only two speeds, fast or inert?

What if we thought of ourselves like the moon and had equal faith in what is ready to fade away and what's invisible as we do in what is shining? What if we could easily shed the known and habitual ways we think of ourselves in order to foster the things within that are in seed form and dormant? What if you gave yourself three days a month or three hours a day to allow everything you know about yourself to disappear, instead of assuming you are falling apart or clinically depressed? What if you broke through your mundane level of thinking and nested yourself in a rich, dark, regenerative soil, where you could be engaged in innocent inquiry with who you are and what you are becoming?

Most of us and our organizations still follow the old mythology, where we are thought of as perpetual motion machines, working at one speed—fast as can be, productive as possible—like stair-climbers in a gym, up, up, up, asking us to exert more effort but getting nowhere very quickly. Ascent, ascent, higher and higher. Never descent, never darkness or a plateau for regeneration.

As a consequence, we become imprisoned in our own rigidities. What if, instead, we realized, like Ram Dass, that we go through many incarnations in this one life? What if we realized that instead of "things" getting better and better if we work harder and harder, that, like a seed, we will each in our own rhythm, go through endless cycles of gestation, birth, growth, death, and renewal?

Like the rest of the natural world, human beings go through seasons. At one point, we are in the full bloom of summer, harvesting, committed, in abundance. Then, naturally, there is an autumnal time of falling away, disillusionment, stagnation, a shedding of what has been used up. Then must come the fallowness and dormancy of winter, death, rest. Eventually, as is happening right outside the windows of this cabin, there is a great melting into muck and mud, which, if one can persevere, opens naturally into an abundant yellow-green time, when everything is possible and horizons open. Consider your own passion for a moment. Is it hiding under the softest fall of snow, or going through a raw shedding? And is your sense of purpose trembling with spring green or flaming in full harvest?

Because we were born into a mechanical metaphor of stasis, most of us self-interrupt in some stage of this cycle. For instance, years ago, whenever I began to experience the stagnation of fall—mental, physical, emotional, or spiritual—I would get stoned. Others may have another cup of coffee, get another mate, house, car, job, or guru. I also avoided internal winter. The only way my system could become dormant was to get very sick. I was living my life as if it were always day, always summer, always up, up, and away.

The truth is we can't escape the movement of our inner seasons. But we all experience them. Some of us go through these cycles of commitment, disenchantment, dormancy, and regeneration in a month. Others may experience a five-year cycle.

My friend, Mary Jane, says each aspect of her being—her heart, mind, spirit, body—have their own separate seasons.

Understanding these cycles, you can come to recognize that when you are feeling disconnected from meaning and mystery, you're moving into fall. This is a signal to begin to turn inward, in order to harvest the wisdom of the last cycle and plant seeds for the next. Winter, or dormancy, can then be welcomed as a time of incubation, rather than stagnation. This natural process, if allowed to occur, fosters trust that the greening of purpose and passion will reemerge from this frozen ground, regenerating your desire to reach out and offer your renewed self.

Continuing for a moment longer with this metaphor for the movement of the life-force, think of yourself as a gardener. You have been given some seeds. You don't actually grow them. You merely provide the conditions in which they can thrive, and then tend them with curiosity and kindness as they grow themselves. You don't explain to the apple tree that it shouldn't be shedding leaves now. Or that it should be producing pears instead, or that its flowers are excessive for the amount of fruit necessary for regeneration. A gardener cultivates a tree by acting on its essential behalf, by making sure it has the necessary spaciousness and support to find opportunities for growth in both darkness and light.

I don't believe that our existence in this world is a random accident. Maybe it is, but I don't believe it. I believe there is more to life that living each day as it comes. The great cellist Pablo Casals agreed. He said that through the whole of recorded history there has never been another such as you.

Each of us is a miracle of uniqueness. Each of us, therefore, is responsible for the discovery of our sustaining passions and rhythms, the cultivation of the green fields in which we can discover what keeps us connected to the full fertility of our soul and all it has to give to the world.

I send you the solidity of these ancient mountains, the width of a blue-violet sky that can hold four weathers simultaneously, the peace of dormancy under a thick winter snow, and the sweetness of spring burgeoning through a thawing soil.

Let us swing wide all the doors and windows
of our hearts on their rusty hinges
so we may learn how to open in love.

Let us see the light in the other and honor it
so we may lift one another on our shoulders
and carry each other along

Let holiness move in us
so we may pay attention to its small voice
and give ourselves fully with both hands.

Inspirations and Appreciations

I am pulled between the force of my appreciation and the hope-less inadequacy of ever truly expressing it:

For the Seeds of Inspiration

Pema Chödrön, *When Things Fall Apart:
Heart Advice for Difficult Times*

Annie Dillard, *Teaching a Stone to Talk*

Milton Erickson, M.D. *The Collected Papers of Milton Erickson*

Victor Frankl, *Man's Search for Meaning*

Thich Nhat Hanh, *Being Peace*

Dee Hock, *Birth of the Chaordic Age*

Sensei Richard Kuboyama

Anne Lamott, *Traveling Mercies: Some Thoughts on Faith*

Anne Morrow Lindbergh, *A Gift from the Sea*

Parker Palmer, *Let Your Life Speak*

Rachel Naomi Remen, *Kitchen Table Wisdom: Stories That Heal*

Meg Wheatley, *A Simpler Way*

David Whyte, *A House of Belonging: Poems*

Ruth First, *A Biography of Olive Shreiner*

For the Blossoms

Because you have changed everything:

Mary Jane Ryan

Andy Bryner

David Peck

Angie McArthur

For the Fruit

Because you give it all meaning:

Ana Li

Stephanie Ryan

Collin and Emily Edwards

Katie Brass

Heather McArthur

The Sapiro Kids

Peris Gumz

Ann Muoser

Anne Powell

Mabel Kuboyama

Lisa Caine

Carolyn Baker

Donald McIlraith

Elaine Goudy

Nathan and Ian Senge

Shelly Glennon

Brian Veivia

Kira and Austin English

Juliy Marie

Jo Pease

June La Pointe

Lawson Drinkard

The Conari Artisans

and to you, the Reader

who has accompanied me, in

kindness, on this journey

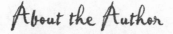

About the Author

Dawna Markova, Ph.D, is internationally known for her ground-breaking work in helping people learn with passion and live on purpose. She is the CEO of Professional Thinking Partners, Inc., cofounder of the Worldwide Women's Web, a former senior research affiliate of the Organizational Learning Center at MIT, and has established learning communities around the world. Her previous books include *The Art of the Possible*, *The Open Mind*; *No Enemies Within*; *An Unused Intelligence*, coauthored with her husband and business partner, Andy Bryner; and, *How Your Child Is Smart*, and *Learning Unlimited*, coauthored with Ann Powell. She is one of the coeditors of *Random Acts of Kindness*™ and *Kids' Random Acts of Kindness*™. Dawna currently lives in the mountains of Utah.

Personal Renewal Workshops

For information on workshops and retreats based on *I Will Not Die an Unlived Life,* go to www.ptpinc.org

To Our Readers

CONARI PRESS publishes books on topics ranging from spirituality, personal growth, and relationships to women's issues, parenting, and social issues. Our mission is to publish quality books that will make a difference in people's lives—how we feel about ourselves and how we relate to one another. We value integrity, compassion, and receptivity, both in the books we publish and in the way we do business.

As a member of the community, we sponsor the Random Acts of Kindness™ Foundation, the guiding force behind Random Acts of Kindness™ Week. We donate our damaged books to nonprofit organizations, dedicate a portion of our proceeds from certain books to charitable causes, and continually look for new ways to use natural resources as wisely as possible.

Our readers are our most important resource, and we value your input, suggestions, and ideas about what you would like to see published. Please feel free to contact us to request our latest book catalog or to be added to our mailing list.

2550 Ninth Street, Suite 101
Berkeley, California 94710-2551
800-685-9595   510-649-7175
fax: 510-649-7190
e-mail: conari@conari.com
www.conari.com